POLITICIANS, PARTISANS, AND PARASITES

POLITICIANS, PARTISANS, AND PARASITES

My Adventures in Cable News

Tucker Carlson

WARNER BOOKS

An AOL Time Warner Company

Warner Books, Inc., 1271 Avenue of the Americas, New York, NY 10020

Visit our Web site at www.twbookmark.com.

 An AOL Time Warner Company

Printed in the United States of America

First Printing: September 2003
10 9 8 7 6 5 4 3 2 1

ISBN: 0-446-52976-1
Library of Congress Control Number: 2003107269

Book design by Fearn Cutler de Vicq

To Susie

Acknowledgments

In addition to my dogs, Agnes and Maisie, who've slept next to my desk through countless magazine pieces and now this book, I'd like to thank:

My cohosts on *Crossfire,* James Carville, Paul Begala, and Bob Novak, who in real life are just the way they appear on television, only more so.

Jim Walton, Teya Ryan, and Sue Bunda at CNN for championing my cause.

Our diabolical *Crossfire* producers and staff, including Sam Feist, Kristy Schantz, Amy Farrar, Kate Farrell, Debbie Berger, Emily D'Alberto, Eileen McMenamin, Abbi Tatton, Chris Rogers, Raeshawn Smith, Josh Cowen, Heather Clapp, Howie Lutt, Stacie Paxton, Joe Van Kanel, Joe Conley, Beverly O'Banion, Chris Youd, James Stubbs, Mike David, Reza Baktar, Doug Koztoski, Jimmy Suissa, Art Thomas, Darren White, and Skip Smith.

The small but valiant team of *Spin Room* commandos: Susan Toffler, Libbie Schlather, Kate Albright-Hanna, and of course my pal Bill Press.

Tammy Haddad, who is always the first person I call, for everything.

Colin Fox, my talented and (remarkably) patient editor at Warner Books.

Binky Urban of International Creative Management, who is every bit as excellent as her reputation.

Matt Labash, the wittiest man in journalism, whose E-mails alone would make a better book than this.

Bill Kristol, Chris Caldwell, Andy Ferguson, David Tell, Richard Starr, Jonathan Last, David Bass, Vic Matus, and everyone else now and once at the *Weekly Standard*.

All the many people in journalism who've been kind to me for no particular reason, especially Adam Meyerson, Paul Greenberg, Bob Sallee, Marion Maneker, Sam Sifton, Tina Brown, Mark Gerson, and Margaret Carlson.

My brother, Buckley, and my parents, Richard and Patricia Carlson, for a lifetime of great dinner table conversation.

And my children, Lillie, Buckley, Hopie, and Dorothy. I hope that when you can read this, it won't embarrass you.

Finally, to the friends, colleagues, and collaborators identified only by pronouns in this book. I've tried to protect you. Sorry I didn't succeed.

Contents

"The trick is to care, but not too much.
Give a shit—but not really."

—*Larry King on success in television*

POLITICIANS, PARTISANS, AND PARASITES

"... in the History of CNN."

✶ ✶ ✶

The best thing about television news is, it's immediate. Everything at a news network happens quickly. Shows are created, canceled, or moved around with no warning, in response to events that no one can predict. It's a completely fluid environment. If you like fluid environments, it's a great place to work. There isn't much waiting around. It takes years to become a doctor or a lawyer, or even a licensed plumber. I became a talk show host in about twelve hours.

It was October 2000, a month before the presidential election. I was reading the paper at home one morning when the phone rang. It was a producer I knew from CNN. "What are you doing after the Cheney-Lieberman debate tonight?" she asked. I couldn't think of anything. "Want to host a new show?"

Why not? I thought. I'd been covering politics for magazines since I left college. Over the previous few years, I'd also done a fair amount of television, though almost always as a guest. I wasn't sure what being a host entailed, but asking questions sounded easier than answering them. Sure, I said. I'll be there.

That night after dinner, I drove over to the CNN bureau in Washington. Dick Cheney and Joe Lieberman had just finished their first and only debate. Outside the auditorium in Danville, Kentucky, flacks from both sides had set up "spin rooms," rapid-response press operations designed to convince the public that their guy had won. Someone at CNN had decided—that very morning, as it turned out—that this might be a good model for a talk show. The name, not surprisingly, was going to be *The Spin Room*.

The idea was to provide immediate analysis of each of the presidential debates. Bill Press, who was already working at CNN as the liberal cohost of *Crossfire,* was going to represent the Left. I was going to represent the Right. We'd critique the candidates' performances, as well as interview professional spinners, like Ari Fleischer from the Bush campaign. To pad out the hour, we'd take calls and E-mails from viewers.

Those were our instructions. At a quarter to midnight, Press and I headed up to the studio. One of the cameramen was sitting on the desk at the Larry King set drinking a Mountain Dew when we walked in. "You got the Reagan chairs tonight," he said. "That's a good sign."

Television networks, like newspapers and magazines, prepare advance obituaries to run when famous people die unexpectedly. To get ready for Ronald Reagan's death, CNN had gone one step further and bought furniture for the blowout coverage it anticipated during the week of the former president's funeral.

These were the chairs. Until now, they'd been in storage. They looked like ordinary chairs to me, but apparently it was considered an honor to use them.

That was comforting, since the chairs were just about all we had. The set amounted to a round, foot-high plywood stage on wheels. The backdrop consisted of a single television monitor on a stand between the Reagan chairs. A graphic in the screen read, *The Spin Room*. The words seemed to be quivering slightly, the way a videotape does when you hit pause on the VCR.

Not very impressive, though considering the short notice, not bad. But the set wasn't the only incomplete part of the show. The writers hadn't finished the scripts, either. Somehow this news never trickled down to me. It came as a surprise.

Twenty minutes into the show, we returned from our first commercial break. "Welcome back to *The Spin Room*," I said, reciting the words as they scrolled up from the bottom of the screen in front of me. Reading from a TelePrompTer isn't difficult, but it takes practice. The machine is run from outside the studio by an operator who pays close attention to the host's lips. The faster you speak, the faster he rolls the script. It works well, until you get tangled up in a word while speaking quickly. With the script moving fast, the rest of the sentence is likely to disappear before you can read it. You'll never find your way back.

I was intent on speaking slowly. So intent, it took me a second to notice that the script had stopped moving. Suddenly there was no script at all, just a piece of advice. Motionless in the screen were the words AD LIB HERE.

It took every ounce of self-control not to repeat the phrase out loud. Unsure of what to do—*make it up* seemed to be the message from the control room—I did my best to look relaxed and unflustered. Then I simply started talking. It worked fine.

Later I was grateful for the experience. On my first night on the air, I'd learned two useful facts about television: Never rely on scripts. ("Ad lib here" is actually pretty good advice.) And when things fall completely apart, attempt to smile calmly and hope no one notices. Usually, no one will.

The rest of the hour was filled with what under normal circumstances would be considered minor catastrophes. At one point, I spent the better part of a minute addressing the wrong camera. In the next segment, I threw to a sound bite that wasn't there. "Take a look at this," I said, pointing my finger at the monitor like a magic wand. Seconds passed. Nothing happened. "Well," I said finally, "let me tell you about it." The moment I began speaking, the tape appeared.

None of it seemed to matter to viewers, who apparently were grateful to see something other than reruns that late at night. The show got CNN's highest midnight rating in memory. The next morning, a network vice president called to offer me a full-time contract. She was enthusiastic about *The Spin Room*'s prospects. If the show continued to prosper over the next two presidential debates, CNN might make it permanent. "This is how *Nightline* started," she said.

Nightline is famous in television, and not just because it's a good program. Thrown on the air by ABC as a special during the Iranian hostage crisis, the show's ratings grew so large so fast that it never went off the air. It was a network programmer's dream, a tiny gamble that paid off big, as well as an inspiration to the entire industry. Ever since, every one-night-only show on television has dreamed of becoming *Nightline*.

The Spin Room, alas, never got there. The show lasted less than a year. It did not win shelves of awards (or any, actually). It did not spawn countless imitators. Twenty years from now, I'm not sure who will even remember that it existed. But I will. It was the weirdest, most amusing job I've ever had.

Shortly after we got word that *Spin Room* was becoming a real show, someone at the network decided that we needed an executive producer to run it. The one we got was named Don. Don had been overseeing *Talk Back Live,* an afternoon call-in show based in Atlanta. He flew in to meet us.

I wasn't immediately impressed. A middle-aged man with perfectly hairless arms, Don was a veteran of years in local news. Maybe because of his background, he came off as both insecure and pompous, the sort of person who uses long words he doesn't fully understand. Moments into our first conversation, he went out of his way to call Larry King stupid. The point was, Don is a whole lot smarter than Larry King. I doubted it.

If producers were cars, Don would not be considered late-model. Still, he had official-sounding credentials. CNN had paid his airfare to Washington. We took his arrival as a sign of our permanence. More than anything, we had hopes Don would make *Spin Room* look better, more network and less cable-access. In retrospect, our naïveté strikes me as almost touching.

One night early on, Don convinced us to run a video clip of giant pandas. You don't see many pandas on political shows, but a pair of them had arrived in Washington that day, so Don figured we could call these pandas newsworthy. Plus, he explained, "People like to see pandas. They're cute. No one ever changes the channel when pandas are on."

We agreed. Unfortunately, Don hadn't bothered to screen the panda tape before the show.

"Welcome back," I said, returning from a commercial break.

"We've got something a little different for you tonight. A pair of giant pandas arrived in Washington this afternoon. They're a gift from the government of China, a kind of peace offering. Here they are."

Bill and I turned to the monitor. The picture came up. There were no pandas. Instead, there was a shot of a cargo plane sitting on the tarmac at Dulles Airport. "Well," I said, "there's the plane. Apparently, the pandas are inside, no doubt tired from the long trip over the Pacific." I looked at Bill.

"Yep, that's one long flight," he said. "Even longer if you're a panda. No movie, no hot towels. Do you think they get little bags of peanuts on board?"

It went on like this. The shot never changed: A plane. On the tarmac. At rest. I wanted to scream at Don. But the show was live, so Bill and I kept chatting.

Finally, after what seemed like hours, the cargo door under the plane opened, and a metal crate appeared. Two workers slowly lowered it to the ground. Then they walked off. And that was it, the extent of the action. If there were pandas in the box—and we repeatedly claimed there were—I never saw them.

After about a minute and a half of this, we dumped out and went to a commercial, smiling the whole time, like it was all part of the plan. The invisible panda plan.

The second we were off the air, Bill went ballistic, holding the microphone to his lips as he screamed at Don. "Hey, Panda Man!" he barked. "I didn't see the pandas you promised. Not one. Not even fur. *Where were the fucking pandas?*"

We didn't pay much attention to Don after that. He spent most of his time in Atlanta. On his occasional trips to Washington, he made the women on our staff nervous. His teeth clicked when he talked, and he told bizarre jokes. He had a disconcerting habit of pointing out people he believed might be Jewish. We didn't miss him when he was gone.

I don't think he missed us, either. Don's main concern seemed to be keeping his job, though it was never clear exactly what that job was. He was known to take naps in his office. During the day he was sometimes unreachable for hours at a time, off somewhere enduring unspecified "dental work." Mostly, he left us alone.

Except, unfortunately, on the air. Don loved chatting into our earpieces during the show. I often got the impression it was the high point of his day. Midway through an interview he'd begin counting us down to the commercial break: "Eight minutes left. Seven-thirty. Seven. Six minutes, thirty seconds." It was odd.

Even more disconcerting was the running commentary. If a guest made a particularly stupid point or wore an unusually ugly tie, Don would comment on it. "That was brilliant," he'd say. Or, "There's a candidate for the rummage sale." He regarded these as droll remarks. I felt like a schizophrenic, doing my best to ignore the voices in my head. It made it hard to do interviews.

If the guest was on the phone, it became impossible. For reasons I never understood, Don's line from the control room overrode the outside phone line. This meant that while Don was speaking through our earpieces, all we could hear was Don. We had no idea what the caller was saying. Sometimes we could guess. Other times we couldn't.

One night, a man called the show to complain about the way the Florida recount was being conducted. He was angry.

"What I don't understand is why they don't just take those ballots and throw them in the trash. I mean, if . . ."

Don cut in. "My, my. Looks like someone should have said 'no' to that second cup of cappuccino tonight. Could be time to switch to decaf." He chuckled at himself, then clicked out.

The man on the phone, meanwhile, was still ranting. ". . . is going to mean to Baker? That's what I want to know."

I didn't know how to answer. Which Baker was he talking about? Senator Howard? Former secretary of state James? The Reverend Jim?

Ultimately, I decided to go with James. Trying to sound confident, I pointed out that after so many years of distinguished public service, Secretary Baker was just the person to oversee the Bush campaign's recount efforts. And while, yes, Baker was a lifelong Republican, he was also a distinguished statesman, and therefore, if not above the partisan fray, then certainly set apart from it.

"Huh?" said the caller, obviously confused. "I'm talking about Baker County, Florida."

If I'd been a little faster, I could have pulled out of the dive before impact: "Of course. But who do you think the county is named after?"

That's what I should have said. As usual, I didn't think of it until after the show. That's the torment of live television. The best lines come to you in the elevator on the way home.

It was a pretty major screwup. To viewers, it must have suggested that at least one of us had a drug problem. (How else could you mistake a county for a retired secretary of state?) We expected to hear from CNN about it. We never did. Nor did we get a response to the panda segment, or to any of the other on-air blunders we were committing with some frequency. Virtually the only time anyone from the network ever called was to inform us that our time slot would be changing. (During its first four months, *The Spin Room* aired at midnight, 1:00 A.M., 11:00, and 11:30, before finally coming to rest at 10:30.) And that was about it.

We had several theories about this. Maybe CNN executives in Atlanta recognized that a new show is bound to have a rocky start and didn't want to spook us by being critical. Or maybe they were so embarrassed by the whole thing they couldn't face up to their mistake by calling us. Or perhaps they simply weren't watching and had no idea what was happening on the show.

Whatever the reason, CNN had given us extraordinary freedom, unheard-of latitude for a daily prime-time show. For half an hour a night, we could do just about anything we wanted. So we did.

Our first goal was to furnish the set. *The Spin Room* a month out looked very much like *Spin Room* the first night: two chairs, a coffee table, and a television monitor on a rolling metal stand. The effect was Early Dentist's Waiting Room, minus the magazines. It was depressing. We weren't the only ones to notice.

One afternoon a package arrived at the bureau, addressed to the show. Inside was a throw rug emblazoned with the Wyoming state flag, and a note from a viewer: "Hope this helps spruce up the set." That night on the air, Bill waved the rug like a banner. We both profusely thanked the donor by name.

Within a week, CNN responded by giving us a network-sanctioned version, a multicolored patchwork rug from Pottery Barn. (Two years later, I noticed, the rug was still in use, brightening the sets of various weekend shows.) We were grateful for the attention, but by then we didn't need it. We were already swamped with furnishings, all sent by sympathetic viewers. We displayed every one of them on the air, thereby inciting people to send more.

And they did. We didn't realize it at the time, but we'd kicked off what amounted to the longest continuous telethon in the history of television. The charity was the show itself.

Within a month, we needed extra space in the office to store all the donations. There were boxes and boxes of them: books, T-shirts, stationery, photographs, self-published manuscripts, paintings, posters, neckties, bow ties, socks, trousers, stuffed animals, candles, picture frames, ashtrays, pins, flags, puzzles, mouse pads, games, magazines, calendars, CDs, LPs, cowboy hats, poetry, assorted taxidermy, chocolate-covered roaches, a case of Mardi Gras beads, countless spinning tops, and a half-dozen doormats with Hillary Clinton's face on them.

There was also a huge amount of food. The rule in television is, never eat anything that comes through the mail. We had trouble following this rule. In addition to crates of barbecue sauces and canned food, we regularly received platters of foil-covered baked goods. At first we tossed them. By the fourth or fifth batch of brownies, this started to seem wasteful. The cameramen were happy to eat anything we passed on. They survived, so we dug in. One night, Bill and I finished off an entire pound of homemade fudge before the show.

We never found a single razor blade in any of it, though I think both of us regretted eating the fudge. One of our producers later speculated that it hadn't been fudge at all, but something called "Velveeta fudge," the result of a chemical reaction between margarine, Nestle Quick, and Velveeta artificial processed cheese food product. (Combine all three in a microwave, and apparently a substance that resembles fudge appears.) In any case, it settled hard. I haven't eaten before a show since.

Bill, meanwhile, preferred to eat on the show. If consuming viewers' food is considered taboo, eating on the air is absolutely verboten. Almost no one does it, because almost no one looks good doing it. Bill didn't care. He'd invent reasons to snack on camera. Shows on animal rights or vegetarianism or weight loss were natural opportunities for food-related props. Bill would grab a burger or a handful of fries and chomp away as he asked his questions. He never seemed happier. He was a natural exhibitionist.

Eating on camera was a metaphor for the way Bill approached life: cheerfully and voraciously. He always wanted a second helping. His appetite for work was almost unbelievable. On a typical day, Bill might wake up with a radio interview, write a column, go for a run, have lunch with friends, finish a book proposal, make thirty calls, bang out a dozen E-mails, do two live shows, and catch a late flight to Hawaii for a weekend speech. On the plane, he'd read two novels and write another column. Monday morning he'd be back in town, ready to do it again. I never heard him complain about being tired. He was an animal. I admired him.

Bill's schedule caught up with him from time to time, and he'd get sick. One night he showed up with a terrible case of the flu. Walking to the studio, he stopped off at the men's room. "Hold on a second," he said, and went inside and threw up. Ten minutes later we were on the air. Bill did the entire show with a trash can between his knees just in case it happened again. He must have felt horrible, but you couldn't tell. He never said a word about it.

My favorite thing about Bill, though, was his willingness to do absolutely anything on the air. In addition to eating, he would sing, wear funny hats, speak French, probably dance on the desk if you asked him to. He was completely, charmingly shameless—literally unembarrassable. In fact, in all the time I worked with him, I think I saw him blush only once.

Ruth Westheimer did it. We had her on one night to talk about politics. Dr. Ruth knows almost nothing about politics, of course. But she does know a great deal about sex, and we strove to do at least one sex-related segment a week, on the grounds that sex was good for ratings, and good ratings were good for us. Plus, sex is fun to talk about.

So on Valentine's Day, we invited Dr. Ruth to answer the deeply irrelevant question: Is there too much sex in Washington or too little? She didn't even bother to respond. Instead, like the hyperaggressive shrink she is, she immediately hijacked the show. "When you get home tonight," she said in her *Hogan's Heroes* accent, "I want the two of you—not together—the two of you with your spouses, I want you to try something new. I want you to try a new position."

How do you respond to an order like that? I didn't know. Bill didn't seem to, either. Before we could think of a snappy comeback, she was off again. "When I watch the two of you," she declared matter-of-factly, "I can visualize what you do in your bedrooms. Did you ever think of that?"

Unlike Dr. Ruth, I had never visualized Bill's bedroom activities, so I had no real idea what she was talking about. But Bill apparently did. He shifted in his chair. Even through his makeup I could see that his face had turned red.

Naturally, we decided to have Dr. Ruth back on as soon as possible. She wasn't exactly breaking news—Elderly Sex Therapist Goes On Talk Show!—but she made for good television. That was our opinion. Others didn't agree. There were some who didn't agree with anything we did.

TV critics, for instance. They didn't care for *The Spin Room,* and said so frequently. A representative review began with the words "amateurish," "sophomoric," and "lightweight," and got more savage from there. One critic compared the program to a "small-market talk radio show." The television writer for Salon.com spoke for many in the professional TV-watching community when he called *The Spin Room* "the worst show in the history of CNN."

There are a lot of ways to take a line like that. Bill and I chose to see the grandeur in it (". . . in the history of CNN"). We wanted to use it in our next ad for the show. There wasn't a chance of that happening. The people who ran the network's promotions department weren't even amused by the idea.

And that's the difference between television and print journalism. When you work in print, a hostile response to your work is considered a sign you may be doing something right. Of course they're upset, goes the reasoning; people always get mad when you tell the truth. It's a rare magazine writer who gets fired for eliciting nasty letters to the editor. I used to take pride in my hate mail. I made a collage out of the nastiest pieces and hung it over my desk.

People don't think like that in television. Television is a purely democratic medium. Success has one measure: the number of people who watch. Nielsen ratings don't make sophisticated distinctions between viewers. Someone who tunes in because he loves the show is worth no more or less than the guy who watches because he's stuck in traction in the hospital and can't find the remote. Every viewer's opinion is equally valid and important. There is pressure not to offend or annoy any of them.

All of this makes television executives exquisitely sensitive to criticism. Smart as they are, none of them is exactly sure what makes a successful show. But they are certain that a bad review will prevent at least some people from watching. Reviews are taken seriously in television. The effect is to give disproportionate power to a small group of TV critics.

It's chilling if you think about it: Hack journalists who spend their days in a darkened room eating ice cream in their undershorts in front of the tube—people who literally watch TV for a living—have influence over your life, career, and paycheck. It's like growing up to find that the kid you picked on in school is now the foreman of your jury. And there's nothing you can do about it.

In the summer of 2002, I got a call from a publicist at CNN. Gail Shister, the television critic of the *Philadelphia Inquirer,* had requested that I speak to the annual convention of the National Lesbian & Gay Journalists Association, of which she was a board member. The convention was on a weekday in Philadelphia, and I was expected to do it for free. It sounded like an unpleasant experience. I've got nothing against gay journalists, but I'm offended by the idea of gay journalists' associations or of any other interest group that attempts to bully news organizations into providing a certain sort of coverage. I didn't want to go.

I knew I had no choice. Shister is an influential critic. Worse, she knows she's an influential critic, and that as a result I would be too intimidated to turn her down. It felt uncomfortably close to blackmail. The publicist agreed that's exactly what it was, but strongly suggested I go anyway. I agreed.

As the date approached, it became clear that my wife was going to deliver a baby on or about the same day I was scheduled to speak. (Our daughter was born while the convention was in progress.) A week before the event, I called the PR department to explain that I wouldn't be able to go to Philadelphia. The publicist reluctantly relayed this news to Gail Shister. Shister responded with a high-volume, obscenity-laden rant. This is an outrage, she said, a completely invalid, stupid excuse and an awful thing to do. She told the publicist that I had better reconsider.

I wasn't going to reconsider. Under any other circumstances, I would have called Gail Shister to tell her so directly. I definitely would have matched her obscenities, maybe even raised her an F-word or two. I didn't do that. Instead, I told the publicist to offer my deepest, most sincere apologies for letting the mere birth of a child prevent me from fulfilling my duty to the National Lesbian & Gay Journalists Association. When I told the story to a friend of mine, a fellow talk show host, he assured me that a man never stands so tall as when he stoops to kiss an ass. But I didn't feel tall. I felt emasculated.

If American TV critics are bad, you'd think Canadian TV critics would be worse, if only because everything in Canada is a shoddy reproduction of its American counterpart. But that hasn't been my experience. The most positive review *Spin Room* ever got came from the *Calgary Herald*. The paper's critic defended our show as witty and important. He genuinely seemed to like it. Looking back, I realize he was probably just grateful.

Nothing makes Canadians happier than the acknowledgment that they exist. I discovered this one night when I said something cutting about Canada. I can't now remember what I said or why I said it, though it's possible I was simply attacking Canada on principle. Friendly as they generally are, Canadians have always made me uncomfortable. There's something a shade off about them. They remind me of the aliens in sci-fi movies who move about undetected among the human population until they're tripped up by some joke or colloquialism they haven't been programmed to understand. ("What do you mean, 'take a leak'?")

I suspect Canadians feel this way about themselves, which is why they're so pleased to be mentioned, even in a nasty way. It confirms that they're real.

Whatever the cause, a lot of Canadians noticed my insult. Scores of them wrote letters and E-mails, and not all to take issue with what I'd said. Many agreed that Canada is indeed a third-rate country. (Masochism is Canada's other notable national trait.) Others just wanted to talk about politics. All expressed themselves in that awkward not-quite-English that is the Canadian language. My favorite E-mail was an attempted sports metaphor meant to describe one of Al Gore's legal setbacks during the Florida recount: "On sixth down and goal to go, Gore just got sacked for a loss of 20 yards."

Soon we had developed a large and loyal base of Canadian fans. None of them counted toward ratings (unfortunately, our three largest demographics—Canadians, college students, and prisoners—went uncounted by Nielsen), but I pandered to them anyway. I intentionally mispronounced the name of their prime minister. I accused them of living in igloos and riding dogsleds to work. I called for an immediate invasion of their country, on the grounds that the United States needs more satellite parking. After a while I began to introduce *The Spin Room* as "the only show on television for and about the people of Canada."

Even at the time, I recognized that a relentless focus on Canada was probably not the best way to win a mainstream audience. On the other hand, I didn't think we were going to win that audience no matter what we did. *Wheel of Fortune* is mainstream. We could never compete. Plus, what's the point of having a television show if you can't indulge your own obsessions?

This was Bill's attitude, too. We were both interested in the free-stuff aspect of the show, but Bill was particularly bold about it. When the network was slow to buy us our own *Spin Room* coffee mugs, Bill took our case directly to the viewers. An artist in California promptly responded with two custom mugs, complete with our portraits painted on them. Bill made certain that at least five minutes a night—an eternity in TV time—was set aside for gifts. He'd hold up the day's most impressive offerings, profusely thank the viewers who sent them, then in effect plead for more. More always came. He would have made a great televangelist.

Bill and I almost never discussed beforehand what we were going to say on the show. We spent hours preparing for our interviews with guests, but the colloquy between us was always unscripted and unrehearsed. Except once. About thirty seconds before the show one night, Bill turned to me and said, "After the open, ask me how my weekend was."

So I did. "I'm so glad you asked," he said. "I spent a wonderful three days in Charleston, South Carolina. What a great town. And what remarkable restaurants." He reached into his pocket and withdrew a handwritten list of the places he'd eaten at over the weekend. He read the name of every one, punctuated with editorial comments like "superb crab cakes. I recommend them. But be sure to make reservations. The place fills up fast."

I never learned what sort of deal Bill had worked with the Charleston restaurant owners, whether his infomercial was payment for meals he'd already eaten, or whether he planned to collect later. Either way, it struck me as a pretty clever arrangement.

I would have tried it myself, but I knew I could never pull it off successfully. Bill has a certain bold panache I lack.

As the weeks wore on, *Spin Room* got progressively weirder, more free-form and self-referential. We continued to heap attention on our Canadian viewers, recite bad poetry, and pronounce words in odd ways. We added a nightly Megalomania Moment, during which we read E-mail from our most slavish fans. We were having such a good time that we hardly noticed the guests, who for the first few months ranged from mediocre to bad. Convincing normal people to go on the air at 10:30 at night is never easy. Our first booker apparently found it impossible. Or maybe she just didn't like us.

Whatever the reason, most of our guests had been culled from the C-list or below. One night we interviewed the editor of a political newsletter with a circulation of "more than 800." (And that estimate was taken from the publication's own promotional literature; I'll bet the real number was a third of that.) I couldn't understand a thing the guy said. Plus, he had a walleye. The next night, we had a woman on from New York who claimed to be an economist. She was almost unbelievable. In addition to having nothing interesting to say, she had a thick foreign accent and a terrible, cringe-making speech impediment.

"I can't believe we had that woman on," I said to Don when we got off the air. "Well, I thought she was very courageous," Don replied. "Her performance gave hope to others with cleft palates."

As the months went on, I waited for some sound of disapproval from on high. We were continuing to solicit more and more stuff from viewers (or as we put it, we were "becoming increasingly interactive with the audience"). CNN is a fairly straitlaced news network, and generally phobic about even the appearance of a conflict of interest. But the call never came. We were scolded only once, on the night we announced the creation of the Jim Traficant Legal Defense Fund. The Ohio congressman had just been indicted on a long list of felony charges, and as talk show hosts we felt it was our duty to help prevent one of the great guests of all time from being locked away beyond the reach of a camera. This, apparently, crossed some line, because after the show an executive from Atlanta called and told us to knock it off.

From time to time we did get directives telling us what language we were allowed to use on the air. It was never clear exactly where they came from—I imagined an Office of Forbidden Words somewhere in the basement of CNN Center—but somehow they filtered down to our producer, who passed them on to us. On the day Linda Chavez withdrew her nomination for secretary of labor after admitting she had employed an illegal alien, we received orders that we were not to utter the phrase "illegal alien." Calling people illegal aliens, our producer explained, "implies that they're different."

Of course they're different, I was about to say, they're illegal aliens. Bill beat me to it. Though he was a committed ideological liberal, Bill had enough respect for language to resist attempts to subvert it. Some of the more overbearing PC regulations clearly annoyed him. His response was two words long: "Fuck that." Once on the air, we went out of our way to explain that Linda Chavez's housekeeper had been both illegal and an alien.

Most of our other run-ins with the language police centered on the word "foreign." At some point many years before, Ted Turner had forbidden the use of "foreign" on CNN. The idea was that, to a global news network, there is no foreign news, only international news. All references to "foreign," therefore, were to be replaced with "international."

It made a kind of abstract sense—more sense certainly than a lot of Turner's decrees—but like all theories about language, it collapsed under the demands of everyday usage. "I have an international object in my eye" didn't sound quite right. Nor did the "French International Legion."

Nor, it turns out, is there any real substitute for "foreigners." The word perfectly captures the reality, as anyone who has watched British soccer fans kick one another to death or seen a Kenyan villager wash down lunch with a cup of hot cow blood can tell you. This isn't international behavior. It's foreign behavior. And the people who do it are foreigners. There's no better way to put it.

And that's exactly how we did put it, again and again. One night we did an entire show—"What the Rest of the World Thinks of the Florida Recount"—designed to highlight just how foreign foreigners really are. No one from CNN complained. Our rare moments of contact with the network's upper management were almost always positive.

One afternoon at the bureau, I ran into Frank Sesno, the Washington bureau chief. He pulled me into his office. "You're about to break out," he said. "I've got two pieces of advice for you. One, remember that I'm the one who found you. Come talk to me from time to time. And, two, people are going to start to recognize you. Don't let it go to your head. Don't become an asshole." I assured him on both counts.

Sesno left CNN before I could come and talk to him again. But I tried to keep my second promise and not become an egomaniac. Unfortunately, it was easy. If anything, the new attention made me feel less confident. Within days of the first show, people whose opinions I had never sought called me to critique my performance on the air. A magazine editor cornered me at a cocktail party in New York and spent twenty minutes explaining how the camera angles on *Spin Room* made me look freakish, like an ugly man in a fun house mirror. "Not flattering," he said. "I'd change them if I were you."

Right away I learned that television brings out the critic in almost everyone. People hardly ever approach print reporters to say, "Gee, I thought your piece was stupid. Not to mention badly written. What an embarrassment." They don't think twice about saying the equivalent to a talk show host. And, of course, sometimes they're right, which is why it's so painful.

Hardest of all to get used to, though, was the loss of anonymity in public. Working in television is like having your picture in the post office. People you've never seen before know what you look like.

I didn't fully comprehend the consequences of this until I flew to Italy for a friend's wedding. Thanks to bad weather, I wound up spending quite a bit of time in the Paris airport. One beer led to another, and by the time I boarded the flight to Florence, I'd definitely been drinking. I wasn't embarrassingly wino drunk, though I was dirty and unshaven. I was, however, impaired enough not to notice that there was a large Moroccan man seated between me and the aisle.

Not long after takeoff, I had to go to the bathroom fairly desperately. (Savvy travelers, I've since learned, don't drink four liters of beer before getting on airplanes.) By this time, the Moroccan guy was asleep, completely passed out and snoring. Rather than wake him, I decided to climb over his seat. Stepping from one armrest to the other, I made it successfully.

I had no such luck on the way back. Years later I convinced

myself that the plane must have hit turbulence just as I was standing over the sleeping man. I'll never know for sure. I do know that somehow I lost my balance and wound up falling knees-first into his lap.

He woke up screaming. I didn't understand the precise meaning of his words, but I got the general point. He yelled in the international language of pain, fear, and confusion. I tried to apologize, but this seemed to make him more agitated. He didn't stop shouting till I got off his lap, which wasn't easy. It was a loud moment.

But not so loud I couldn't hear my own name, spoken in a stage whisper from three rows back. It was a group of American tourists. They were staring at me. "That's definitely him," said one. "I saw him on CNN last week."

It didn't take long to conclude that drinking in airports isn't worth the trouble. I had a harder time making the same decision about smoking.

I never had any serious intention of giving up cigarettes. I'd smoked since I was thirteen, and with every passing year I liked it more. There wasn't much incentive not to like it. Smoking is common and accepted in the magazine business. During my five years at the *Weekly Standard,* I smoked at my desk all day every day, two packs or more of Camel regulars.

Pro-health propaganda never once detracted from my enjoyment of tobacco. If anything, it only steeled my resolve to pollute myself. When I was in high school, there was a much-aired public service ad that opened with two kids sitting on a playground. The older one produces a joint, lights it, and tries to pass it to the younger boy. "Come on, Bobby," he coos in the most sinister possible way, "take a hit." No, says Bobby resolutely, putting up his hand. "Only dopes do dope." The older kid looks disgusted. "I thought you were *cool,*" he snorts.

The moral, I guess, was supposed to be that Bobby did the right thing in the face of peer pressure. The moral I took away from it was, Bobby is a dork.

The one time I tried to quit smoking cigarettes, I did my best to empathize with Bobby. There's nothing cool about hurting your body, I told myself. About two months later, I had to face the horrible truth: The antitobacco people are lying. Smoking really is cool. And I'm less cool for not doing it.

So I started again. Which was probably inevitable. The main problem with quitting is not the physical withdrawal. Even the most addicted smoker stops berating his loved ones after half a year or so. The problem is that unlike, say, a sex-change operation, becoming a nonsmoker is reversible. You're always a convenience store away from relapse.

If it weren't for television, I'd probably still be smoking. Smoking isn't popular in TV. Hardly anyone in the industry does it. (For years under Ted Turner, CNN employees were not allowed to smoke, on or off the job.) Cigarettes are not welcome on the set, and it's a long and inconvenient walk from the studio to the curb out front. I probably could have learned to live with this, much as I hate looming around the entrances to buildings. But what I couldn't handle was the reaction from viewers.

After seventeen years of smoking, of course, I was used to getting health advice from strangers. "Don't you know that's bad for you?" they'd say, pointing to my cigarette. I'd give my stock response ("You've got to be kidding!" in deadpan mock horror) and walk away smiling. It never bothered me.

Suddenly, the dynamic was different. People who recognized me from television always seemed stunned when they saw me smoking in public. "You *smoke?*" they'd say. I searched for a snappy comeback—"Only after sex" or "Just started today" or "Yes, but I don't inhale"—but I could never bring myself to deliver it. The disapproval was too strong. They sounded shocked and deeply disappointed, like I'd been arrested for doing something creepy in a men's room. They treated me like Pee Wee Herman.

I never understood exactly why. Maybe I don't look like the sort of person who would smoke, and they found it disturbing to find out that I am. Or maybe viewers of cable news just don't like cigarettes. I still don't know. But I quit anyway. Weary of the battle, I surrendered and allowed the dark forces of Health to claim victory over my personal life.

★   ★   ★

Eight months into the show, despite countless requests and as many subsequent promises, we still didn't have official, CNN-supplied *Spin Room* coffee mugs. Both Bill and I were bothered by this, and not just because we were strongly in favor of free stuff. Mugs make good gifts. It was hard enough getting decent guests to leave dinner in time for a 10:30 show. It would have been nice to send them away with a souvenir.

More important, there was a principle at stake. Every talk show has mugs. By definition. You can sit around a desk and talk. You can beam that conversation by satellite into living rooms around the word. You can even give the whole thing a name and a regular time slot. But if the network hasn't come up with official mugs, it's not a show.

That was our argument anyway. It wasn't taken very seriously by the Givers of Mugs at CNN.

One morning in May, I woke up determined to get mugs. Don was no help—"I'd like one myself if you get them," he said—so I called around the network. I wound up on the phone with a woman named Leslie in the PR office. She was friendly enough, though there was an odd strain in her voice. She sounded nervous. She was sorry about the mugs, she said; there wasn't much she could do. "I don't think mugs are in your budget."

Two-dollar mugs *aren't in the budget?* I lost control. Within seconds, I'd launched into a high-volume lecture about how it was this very attitude—this small-minded, reactionary, bureaucratic legalism—that had made Soviet Communism a living hell for millions. She listened politely. Then she gave me a number for the CNN gift shop in Atlanta. "Maybe they can help." I called right away. The number had been disconnected.

I should have caught the hint.

But I didn't, partly because I was busy. Bill and I were taping the show that afternoon so we could have dinner with our boss, Sid Bedingfield, the general manager of CNN, who had flown up from Atlanta to see us. Sid hadn't mentioned what he wanted to talk about. I didn't spend a lot of time wondering. He'd sounded normal on the phone.

He didn't look normal at the restaurant. He and Bill were sitting in a corner booth. Even from ten feet away I could tell something was wrong. Sid didn't make me wait to find out. He dropped the hammer immediately. "I've got some bad news," he said, still shaking my hand. "We're canceling *Spin Room.*"

My first thought was, So this is why we never got our mugs.

Sid spent a couple of minutes explaining why the show was being pulled. I can't recall his exact words—I'd ordered a martini by this point, the first and last of my life—but it was something about how the time had come for our careers to take new, better, more sensible directions. We've done this for your own good, was the general idea.

I listened, though not very carefully. Even as I watched my job disappear, I couldn't shake my mug obsession. When Sid paused, I asked him: Did Leslie from PR know this was going to happen? Yep, he said.

It was like a flashback from my childhood. When I was little, my father worked in television in Los Angeles. Every fall, he went to his favorite men's store to get measured for a new on-air wardrobe, compliments of ABC. One year, right around contract negotiation time, the suits didn't come.

Annoyed, my father called the store. Then he called back. Finally he got through to the tailor. Hurry up and deliver the suits, he said. "There are no suits," said the tailor. "I was told not to make them. You've been fired."

The tailor turned out to be right. I was in the first grade when it happened, and although my dad always seemed more amused than upset by the experience, I remember being shocked when I heard about it. Even then I wondered: What sort of weird business is it where the guy who makes your clothes knows more about your future than you do?

Twenty-five years later, I finally understood. Sooner or later, just about everyone in television gets canned, usually without warning. As Sid pointed out, there's no reason to take it personally. "Someday it will happen to me, too," he said.

King's Law of Detachment

✳   ✳   ✳

*T*he *Spin Room* was pulled off the air immediately. There was no farewell show, no warning to viewers that the program was being canceled and wasn't coming back. On Monday, it just wasn't there. For weeks, the office continued to receive gifts in the mail, as well as a flood of letters from bewildered and distraught Canadians.

Meanwhile, I moved to *Crossfire,* CNN's oldest political debate show. Mary Matalin, the primary conservative host, had left to work in the Bush White House. I took her place, alternating with Bob Novak, a seventy-year-old columnist who had been doing the show on and off since the early 1980s. Bill Press remained the cohost on the Left. I'd always liked *Crossfire.* I was grateful to have the job.

Not everyone was grateful I got it. Congressman Tom DeLay of Texas, the House Republican whip, loudly complained that I was too liberal to represent the Right on the air. (As DeLay's spokeswoman put it to the *New York Post,* I was "not a real Republican.") Bob Novak voiced the same complaint.

The accusation wasn't true (on many issues, I was more conservative than anyone who had ever hosted the show). But it was enough to make me worry about losing my job. CNN was then engaged in a well-publicized ratings battle with Fox News Channel. The conventional view was that Fox was gaining because cable news viewers are disproportionately conservative. Conservatives like to watch conservatives, and Fox had a greater number of conservative hosts than CNN.

That was the theory. I don't know if it was accurate. I do know that a lot of people at CNN believed it. Being called a secret liberal was a serious charge. It suggested that my presence would harm *Crossfire* ratings. It made me sound like a poseur, or at the very least a lightweight who didn't know what he believed. It provided more ammunition to those who claimed that CNN skewed to the left. I felt smeared. Not that there was much I could do about it, short of punching out Tom DeLay. And, mad as I was, I realized that would probably be counterproductive.

In the end, I tried to keep in mind the best piece of advice I ever heard about working in television. It came from Larry King. At the 2000 Democratic Convention in Los Angeles, King came up to me in a hallway, took my arm, and with no preface said, "Let me tell you something about this business. The trick is to care, but not too much. Give a shit—but not really." He looked at me for a second, then walked away.

I've tried to live by King's words ever since, mostly out of an instinct for self-preservation. Television is a less predictable business than most, because so many basic elements of it are beyond human control. You can't make people watch your show. Most of the time you can't even know for sure why viewers prefer one show to another. Getting ratings isn't just not a science. It's not even an art. It's a guess. At best.

Yet everything hangs on ratings. You can imagine the tension and uncertainty and blind superstition that result. Why do network entertainment divisions immediately churn out cut-rate clones of their competitors' successful shows, even though most of the copies will fail miserably? Because they don't know what else to do.

In an environment like this, it's best not to link your sense of self too closely to the success of whatever show you happen to be working on. It could all end tomorrow, and likely will. Still, it's hard not to get emotionally involved. For most people in television, King's Law of Detachment is an unattainable goal. It takes a different kind of person to truly not care too much.

A little less than a year after *Spin Room* was canceled, Bill Press was on his way out at CNN. One day he was informed that he would no longer be hosting *Crossfire*. The news came without much warning and with almost no explanation. I never understood what Bill had done wrong, and I don't think he did, either. But he accepted the news in a characteristically dignified way, and he rebounded quickly. Within weeks, he had signed with MSNBC to host another show. We never stopped having dinner together.

With Bill gone, *Crossfire* changed completely, remade for the first time in twenty years. The format was expanded to an hour.

The set was moved from a studio at the CNN bureau on Capitol Hill to a 250-seat auditorium at George Washington University downtown. And the program got two new cohosts on the Left: James Carville and Paul Begala.

Carville and Begala were longtime political consultants, most famous for their work on the 1992 Clinton campaign. Both were from the South (Begala from Texas, Carville from Louisiana), and both were born debaters—sharp and fast and relentlessly opinionated.

Of the two, however, only Begala had actually hosted a television show. No one worried about Carville's ability to do it; he was obviously a natural performer. But just to be safe, the network's vice president in charge of talk shows wanted to brief him on some of the mechanics involved. Ten days before the launch of the new show, she set up a meeting at West 24, a restaurant Carville then had in Washington. It was supposed to be a "working lunch." As distinct from, say, a drinking lunch.

By the time I arrived a little after noon, Carville had finished his bourbon and was working on a glass of wine. We chatted until the food came; then the executive from CNN began to tell Carville what it's like to work in television. You won't have any problems, she said sweetly. But since you've never done it before, there are a few things you should probably know.

Carville stared at his plate as she spoke. She was just getting to the part about the tricks of the trade when Carville suddenly looked up and began shaking his head vigorously from side to side. The executive stopped talking, confused. "You made a big mistake hiring me," Carville shouted, sounding very agitated. "I can tell you that. A BIG mistake. Because I don't give a shit. I don't. So what are you going to do? Fire me? Go ahead. I don't care. In fact, I'd like it. I don't want this job anyway."

I decided later that this was Carville's Prison Chow Line Moment, the violent fit that every savvy inmate throws the first time someone tries to cut ahead of him in the cafeteria. The idea is, if you show them you're a complete psycho the first day, they'll never bother you again.

Carville's moment lasted longer than most. On his very first night on the air, he went out of his way to personally attack Dick Parsons, the chairman of AOL Time Warner, and hence Carville's ultimate boss. While acting as the cochairman of Bush's Social Security Commission, Carville charged, Parsons had "fraudulently misrepresented facts to his fellow black Americans." Carville said this while looking directly into the camera. Then he grinned.

I soon came to revise my view of Carville's motives. He wasn't pretending not to care in order to make a point or to strengthen his bargaining position. There was nothing phony about his outrageousness. He actually didn't care. For real. And it was clear he was having a great time not caring.

Night after night, Carville cheerfully ignored many of the basic conventions of television. He'd pause midway through reading a script to wonder aloud what it meant. If a producer said something through his earpiece that annoyed him, he'd say so on the air: "Huh?" or "What are you talking about?" or "I don't want to do that." On those occasions when the producer won the debate, Carville would mention that, too: "Our producer wants us to use CNN polls, so here's one."

Carville appeared almost completely unaffected by being on camera. His Louisiana accent was as thick as ever. (Transcripts of Carville shows were always studded with "UNINTELLIGIBLE" in place of sentences the transcribers couldn't make out.) He flamboyantly mispronounced the names of guests, sometimes adding or removing multiple syllables at a time. He wore jeans and belched at the audience during commercial breaks. He got away with it all, mostly because he seemed so natural doing it.

One night, as we were sitting on the set waiting for the show to begin, Carville seemed to forget completely that there was anyone else around. In fact, there were hundreds of people in the auditorium, some of them seated just ten feet away. Carville leaned across the table toward me, the way you do when you're sitting in a booth in a crowded restaurant. "Do you ever have sexual fantasies?"

I wasn't sure if people in the audience could hear. I knew people in the control room could. We were both wearing open microphones. Every word was being carried to an untold number of listeners around CNN, none of whom we could see. It was like sitting on the wrong side of a one-way mirror.

I gave as vague an answer as I could muster: "Well, I think that, uh, like most people, you know, I—"

He cut me off. "Well, I have them," he said. He then described one. In detail. Complete with hand gestures. Out of the corner of my eye I caught a glimpse of the audience. The people in the front row were transfixed.

Carville, meanwhile, had left this world, transported into another X-rated dimension by the vividness of his imagination. His eyes had a distant look. His face was contorted into a snarling leer. He was slapping the air with both hands.

At this point, our producer, who obviously hadn't been paying attention, started yelling through my earpiece. "Tucker! Can you hear me? Can you hear me? Stop him. Get him to shut up. You have GOT to get him to stop talking about this. Change the subject. Do anything. Please. Everyone in the control room can hear what he's saying. Someone's going to make a tape of this. Please."

Carville could tell by my face that something was going on. "Is that Sam?" he said, obviously annoyed. "Is that Sam Feist, our corporate butt-boy producer? Sam, if you can hear me, lighten up."

It was at that moment that James Carville became one of my favorite people.

Not that I didn't sympathize with Sam. Part of any producer's job is to try to keep the hosts moving in the same direction and to prevent them from wandering off into dangerous territory—to be, in effect, the show's troop leader. Carville was not a compliant Cub Scout. He was all id, a wild man, the only person I've ever encountered whose personality had to be toned down for television. None of it was an act.

I'm always amazed by how many people assume that talk show hosts are merely pretending to be outraged or interested in the things they talk about. "You don't really believe all that, do you?" I've been asked the question dozens, maybe hundreds of times, always by liberals. Liberals have trouble believing that anyone who disagrees with them politically could be a decent person. Once they decide they like you, they assume you must be a liberal, too—in my case, a closet liberal.

I set them straight right away. Actually, I say, I believe every bit of it, sometimes more than I say on the air. They hate hearing this, but it's true. In fact, I do believe everything I say. You have to. Arguing a position you don't really support is a sure way to wind up loathing yourself. Plus, genuine conviction makes for a good debate. Phoniness is easy to spot.

Which is not to say I don't have occasional doubts. There are plenty of issues I don't have strong feelings about. There are plenty more that are easier to defend in the abstract than in real life. Take the controversy over whether the Confederate flag should be displayed in public settings. For a lot of white people in the South, the Confederate battle flag is a symbol of a noble heritage and culture. When they see the stars and bars, they don't think of slavery or Jim Crow. They think of their ancestors.

I understand this. Wanting to have the Confederate flag flown over the South Carolina statehouse doesn't make you a racist, any more than wearing green on St. Patrick's Day makes you a supporter of IRA pub bombings. Generalizations to the contrary—like most stereotypes about white southerners—are more a form of cheap snobbery than an argument: "They're conservative. They talk funny. They probably like deer hunting and NASCAR. They must be bigots." It's unfair. I'm annoyed by it.

But it's still difficult to defend the Confederate flag. For one thing, the Confederates were traitors who fought a war against their own country. For another, the flag offends black people. Maybe it shouldn't, but it does. Many black people do think of segregation when they see the Confederate flag. Why should a black person have to be confronted with a symbol he finds deeply offensive every time he walks into a public building that he helps pay for with his tax dollars? I don't want to see a portrait of Louis Farrakhan every time I go to my statehouse. The average black South Carolinian shouldn't have to see the Confederate flag every time he goes to his.

Maybe because I'm not from the South, I didn't have an opinion about the Confederate flag until I started working on *Crossfire*. One benefit of hosting a talk show is that it forces you to learn about, and take a position on, virtually everything that happens in the news. That's also the downside. The more you learn about a subject, the more complicated it becomes, and so, inevitably, do your views on it. From "complicated," it's a short trip to "nuanced." Nuance, needless to say, is the enemy of clear debate.

This is where the producer comes in. A good producer can smell nuance from a hundred yards. He can sense when you've let doubt or details fog the spotless clarity of your own position. He knows when you're starting to question the basic rightness of your case. That's when he begins his pep talk.

"Look," he'll say calmly, "no one expects you to defend what McVeigh did. Obviously. That's indefensible, and it would be wrong. You wouldn't do it. You're just making the point that it's not the government's business how many blasting caps you buy or how much ammonium nitrate fertilizer you stockpile. It's your right to have that stuff, as an American. That's what the Second Amendment was written to protect. That's why George Washington led men into battle to die. That's what freedom is all about. So I don't think you need to worry about looking like you're endorsing what happened at Oklahoma City. What you're doing is taking a stand against Big Brother."

Sometimes it works. There's almost no political position that can't be justified on grounds of liberty or compassion: We have a right to do this; we have an obligation to do that. Armed with just these two arguments, a good producer can make almost any half-baked proposal sound like The Right Thing to Do. Many times I've listened through the wall of my office as a producer gives the pep talk to my cohost in the next room ("You're for seat-belt laws because seat-belt laws save lives"), only to get the inverse spiel myself moments later ("Since when is it government's job to protect you from yourself?").

A skillful talk show producer is like the corner man in a boxing match. His job is not to keep you from getting hurt; it's to help you perform, to buck you up, whet your desire for blood, and in general whip you into a controlled frenzy.

As long as you remember that your interests and his don't always intersect—what's good for ratings is not necessarily good for your career—there's nothing wrong with the arrangement. It's useful. It's also straightforward. Producers may lie, but at least their motives are easy to understand.

No matter what critics say, television producers are generally not political partisans. Like most journalists, they tend to be liberal in a vague way, but their main ideology is ratings. A producer is committed to whatever political philosophy makes the most compelling TV. Marion Barry–Jerry Springer is every talk show producer's dream ticket for president, followed closely by Alan Dershowitz–Don King and Jim Traficant–O. J. Simpson. A good producer votes the story. No matter what the story happens to be.

One night on the air, I revealed this. During a segment on reality TV, I described television producers as "diabolical." It didn't strike me as a particularly controversial thing to say. It was as close to an unadorned statement of fact as I could get. And I'd meant it in the most affectionate way.

Our producer saw it differently. The moment we went to a commercial, he was in my ear. " 'Diabolical'? Why do you always say that?" He sounded offended. "Because it's true," I said. Twenty minutes later, we came to the end of the show. I looked over to my TelePrompTer for the usual wrap-up: "Good night from *Crossfire*. Stay tuned for *Connie Chung Tonight*." At the end of the script was a new line: "And remember: Television producers are not diabolical."

I couldn't read it. It was simply too big a lie. Outside of the Saudi royal family, TV producers are probably the most

Machiavellian group on the planet. But that doesn't stop me from liking them. They tend to be witty and interesting and good at what they do. The best ones are as creative as any filmmaker, and much less appreciated. Some of them are exceptionally smart.

Sam Feist, the *Crossfire* head producer, is as canny as anyone I've ever met in business or politics. He's a smoother diplomat than most career employees at the State Department. And he's sharp. While working full-time at CNN, he got a law degree from Georgetown night school, then took and passed the bar exam. He never intended to practice law. He just admired the systematic way lawyers think.

For raw mental horsepower, though, it's hard to top the research staff. We once had a researcher at *Crossfire* who could instantaneously produce facts about almost anything: The chief export of Zanzibar. The number of congressional districts in Pennsylvania. The average SAT score at the University of Illinois, Champaign-Urbana campus. If she didn't know the answer off the top of her head, she could find someone who did, usually in under a minute.

It was a remarkable skill. After a while we treated it like a party trick. She was like the roommate who can flip his eyelids inside out or the guy who can fit a dollar's worth of quarters up his nose. We'd ask her pointless questions purely for the pleasure of hearing the answers: What was Larry Flynt's second wife's name? How many burglaries were committed in Boston last year? What was the closing line of Gerald Ford's last State of the Union Address? What did Bill Clinton really believe in?

We stumped her on the last one (it was unanswerable), but she got the rest in the time it takes to make a sandwich. Sometimes I wondered why she was working for us. Shouldn't you be teaching a class or something? That's what I wanted to ask her. I came close once, the time I saw someone order her—without saying please—to hurry up and fetch him a cup of coffee. But I kept quiet. She was too good to lose.

I respect producers, but even if I didn't, I'd have a hard time ignoring them. Producers tend to produce, which means telling you what to do while you're trying to talk to somebody else on the air. Most of the time it's helpful. Some of the time, as Don, *The Spin Room* producer, repeatedly proved, it's not. Knowing which is which is the trick, and that's harder than it sounds. Even the most arrogant talk show host instinctively defers to an authoritative voice. All human beings do. Succeeding in television requires learning how to disregard a producer's directions and, instead, do what seems right at the time. It took a plane crash for me to figure this out.

Three weeks after September 11, I left on a trip to Pakistan. My plan was to make it over the border into Afghanistan at the Khyber Pass by the time the war started and write about the experience for *New York* magazine. As it turned out, I never got out of Pakistan, though I had an interesting and fruitful time anyway.

After ten days or so, I had to head back to *Crossfire*. My plane home left at night from Islamabad, stopped in Peshawar at the Afghan border, then went on to Dubai, in the United Arab Emirates. Because of the bombing campaign in Afghanistan, the normal route had been doubled in length. A trip that usually takes two hours was going to take nearly four. I could tell right away it was going to be a bad flight.

Every Pakistan International Airways flight opens with a prayer. Chanted in Arabic over the PA system, it suggests a God-only-knows-whether-we'll-land-safely attitude. It does not inspire confidence. I would have ordered a drink, but none are permitted on PIA, though heavy smoking at all times is allowed, even encouraged. Ten minutes into the flight, everyone seemed to have a lit Marlboro and a cup of black coffee. It reminded me of an AA meeting.

Once we landed in Peshawar, forty or fifty new people got on the plane, far more than could fit in the remaining seats. These were friends and family of the passengers and crew. They'd come on board to say hello. Groups of people squatted in the aisles chatting until it was time to take off again. After we were airborne, I headed to the men's room. The cockpit door was open. Several men were sitting cross-legged on the floor, smoking and talking with the pilots. Post 9-11 security paranoia had not yet reached PIA.

I returned to my seat and tried to read. About twenty minutes out of Dubai, over the Arabian Sea, something dramatic and very loud happened to the airplane. I still don't know what it was. It felt like we'd hit a building. I could hear something large ripping off the undercarriage. The plane shuddered, dropped, then halfway recovered. We were still flying, but sideways, listing like a wounded bird.

A Croatian war photographer who was sitting next to me asked a member of the crew what was going on. "Everything is fine," the man said, then disappeared into the galley. No one believed him. Everyone on board knew we were going to crash.

A few minutes later, we did. Despite the obvious damage to the plane, the pilot attempted to land. It didn't come close to working. We bounced off the runway into a sand dune and kept going. We seemed to be moving incredibly fast. I braced my feet against the seat in front of me as the airplane skidded and hopped. It was black outside, and through the window I could see a shower of sparks coming from the right wing, which had snapped and was dragging along the ground. The lights went out. The plane came to rest at a steep angle, on its side.

My first thought was, I have got to get off this airplane. Jumping out of my seat, I made it to the front exit and tried to open the door. It was jammed, held fast by the twisted fuselage. I was just about to take a running leap at it when a crew member— the same person who had assured us that "everything is fine"— grabbed my arm. "Return to your seat," he said. "The captain has not called for us to exit the aircraft."

We hadn't heard from the captain one way or the other, and never did. Maybe he was injured. Maybe he'd assumed the fetal position on the floor of the cockpit. Most likely, he'd already escaped out the front window and was jogging through the sand toward the lights of Dubai. In any case, he wasn't around. He definitely wasn't issuing directions.

I pulled loose from Everything-Is-Fine Guy and made another assault on the door. This time it popped open. The rubber slide inflated instantly (quite a sight), I jumped on it (quite a ride), and was gone. It took me about a minute to stop running.

Investigators never figured out why the plane, which was burned, didn't erupt into a ball of fire. There were quite a few injuries, but everyone survived, no thanks to the efforts of the flight crew. I came away reminded of something that every American (but apparently not every Pakistani) knows from growing up in a free country: If you know what to do, don't wait for instructions.

The same principle applies to hosting a talk show. As the host, it's up to you to decide what happens on the show. And no matter what the producer says, you have the power to do it. Contrary to popular belief, most talk shows do not have five-second delays. If you say something, viewers will hear it. On a live show, there's no intervening authority between your microphone and television sets around the country.

Carville proved this one night by using the word "assholes" on the air. He was talking about the September 11 hijackers ("those assholes!" he shouted), so it was hardly a controversial sentiment. Some viewers were offended by it anyway, and I'm sure the producers would have preferred that he expressed his feelings differently. But at the crucial moment, the producers' opinion didn't matter. Only Carville had control over what Carville said. Carville wanted to call the hijackers "assholes."

I've never used one of the Seven Forbidden Words on television, though I have occasionally become personal and nasty with a guest. Getting personal is probably more offensive to a lot of people (including me) than swearing. I hate doing it. I feel bad afterward. But on *Crossfire,* it's sometimes almost impossible to resist.

By its nature, *Crossfire* can be a tense show. People are arguing about emotional subjects under strict time pressure in a public forum. Everyone is highly caffeinated. No one wants to look stupid. Tempers can flare.

Mine tends to flare in the presence of party hacks. They annoy me. Being a blind partisan defeats the whole purpose of being an adult. Once you grow up, you're meant to develop your own grown-up opinions about things. You're supposed to disregard what Mommy says and say what you really think. Some people can't handle this. They want to be bossed around and told what to believe. They want to take orders. They're only comfortable expressing preapproved thoughts. Reflexive party loyalty was made for people who miss Mommy's firm hand.

This would merely be sad if it didn't also breed deception. Partisanship is groupthink, the enemy of truth. I once had a friend who was close to Bill Clinton. One morning during the impeachment trial, he let me listen in to the daily conference call of Clinton defenders. There were probably fifteen people on the line: lawyers, political consultants, and professional flacks. I knew almost all of them. They were the people you saw on television day after day attacking Ken Starr as a right-wing monster and assuring the rest of us that whatever Clinton did, it surely didn't "rise to the level" of anything really bad. This was the call where they learned what to say.

Here was a group of smart people, most with Ivy League degrees and impressive jobs, lining up to receive their lies, exaggerations, and half-truths for the day. They planned to take this pap—the "message"—out in public, where they'd repeat it unthinkingly but with great passion, thereby humiliating themselves in front of America. And they were doing it all so someone else wouldn't have to suffer for a mess he created. It was selfless in a way. I found it sickening.

It reminded me of the scene in *Animal Farm* where the pigs repaint the slogans on the side of the barn and expect all the other animals to pretend they've never changed. When you're a partisan, you're the other animals. The party tells you what to do, and you do it. You take directions. You obey. It's like being in the Army, without the nobility. You're an orderly, the weakest guy in prison, somebody else's errand boy. You're not a man.

Not surprisingly, your superiors have no respect for you. Leaders always hold contempt for those they dominate, and politicians are no exception. Has a politician ever really cared about a staffer? Yet political leaders expect—require—their followers to display absolute devotion in return. Bill Clinton's defenders often boasted about their "loyalty" to the president. But it was obvious—glaringly, embarrassingly obvious—that Clinton had no loyalty to them. He dropped them when they became inconvenient, disavowed them when it suited his purposes.

Still they kept defending him, even when it was clear to everyone they'd been used. Maybe people like this think they're upholding some sort of higher ideal by debasing themselves. (If so, I'd love to know what the ideal is.) Maybe they're just masochists. I'm not a shrink, so I don't understand the psychology. I do know that I have as much contempt for these people as their own bosses do, and when they come on my show, I'm apt to lose my temper.

Ideologues, by contrast, almost never make me mad. No matter how crackpot the opinion, I can respect a deeply held view. I may not believe the earth is flat, but if you sincerely do, I won't hate you for it. We've had a lot of true believers on *Crossfire*. I don't think I've ever yelled at one. Secretly, I admire many of them.

I even have affection for poor old wild-eyed Bob Smith of New Hampshire. Smith was a Republican senator who in 1999 suddenly realized that the GOP wasn't living up to its own principles. This came as such a complete shock to Smith that he left the Republican party and became an independent. But before he did, Smith gave one of the more memorable speeches ever delivered on the Senate floor. He began by doing something cruel: He read portions of the Republican platform out loud.

Except possibly at conventions, platforms are not meant to be read in public, much less studied, followed, or even paid attention to. Platforms are designed to be ignored. Everyone in Washington understood this. Except Bob Smith.

"As a first step in reforming government," Smith thundered, reciting the painfully hopeful words of some unnamed party scribe, "we support elimination of the Departments of Commerce, Housing and Urban Development, Education, and Energy." Whatever happened to that promise? Smith wanted to know. Or to the promise to defund Legal Services? Not to mention public broadcasting, the United Nations, and the National Endowment for the Arts. And where's the legislation that would "make clear that the Fourteenth Amendment's protections apply to unborn children"? After five and a half years of Republican control of Congress, Smith demanded, where is any of it?

"The Republican platform," Smith concluded, "is a meaningless document that has been put out there so that suckers like me and maybe suckers like you out there can read it."

Smith's speech went on for close to an hour. For the duration, he howled like a man deceived, the lone member of the Senate Sucker Caucus. Watching it, you got the feeling Smith was the last guy on his block to learn the horrible truth about Santa Claus.

The whole experience seemed to drive him right off the rails. Not long afterward, Smith announced he was going to run for the White House. I called him to see if he was serious. He was. "I'm going to be president of the United States," he told me with what sounded like complete certainty. "I really believe that. I feel very confident about this. I'm absolutely convinced I can win. I wouldn't do it if I wasn't. I think young people are going to be joining this campaign by the millions."

Unfortunately, the young people never came. Neither did their parents. Smith's campaign tanked after several painful, dispiriting months. He crawled back to the Republican party, but the damage was done. His colleagues—the ones who had written then ignored the party platform—never fully accepted him again. He was beaten in the GOP primary two years later.

Bob Smith's career came to a sad end, and there was never any doubt that it would. Smith wasn't cut out for politics, which tends to turn even the most realistic candidates slightly delusional. He would have fared even worse in television. If running for office encourages you to imagine millions of supporters, hosting a show can entirely separate you from reality.

★   ★   ★

I didn't have a lot of respect for Jesse Jackson before I saw him host a television show, but I had even less after. It was in the mid-1990s, when Jackson still had his own low-rated weekend program on CNN called *Both Sides with Jesse Jackson*. The show had been a gift from Ted Turner, who apparently had decided that Jackson wasn't getting enough media exposure. Or something. I never got the details.

I was there to talk about the CIA and cocaine smuggling. Jackson and others were alleging that the CIA had helped bring crack to inner-city Los Angeles ten years before, supposedly as a way to fund the Contra war in Nicaragua. I had written an article that week calling the charges ridiculous. The show was going to be a kind of debate, with Jackson moderating, as well as advocating a position. (This, presumably, was what the producers meant by *Both Sides*.)

As we chatted before the show, I was struck immediately by how little Jackson seemed to know about the topic. He was almost totally ignorant of the facts of the story, even though as a public figure calling for a Congressional investigation into the CIA, he was part of it. He kept confusing the key players. He mispronounced virtually everyone's name. He clearly had no idea what he was talking about. I almost challenged him to summarize, in five sentences or less, what he thought the CIA had done wrong. But I was there as a guest, so that seemed rude.

Then the lights came up, and something amazing happened: Jackson became knowledgeable. His questions were crisp and direct. So were his follow-up questions. Nothing rhymed. Suddenly, he seemed to have a grasp of the story.

It took me a minute to figure out what had happened. Not only had Jackson's staff prepared all of his questions, printing them out and pasting them to the five-by-eight blue cards that are ubiquitous in television, but, I saw when I looked closely, they had also prepared his *answers*.

"Isn't it true, Mr. Carlson, that the CIA . . . ," a scripted question might begin. Beneath it, in large type, was what Jackson's staff hoped would be a suitable reply to the answer: "But, Mr. Carlson, how can you say that, given that . . . ?"

It was all there on the cards. As long as the conversation didn't stray into the completely unexpected, Jackson was fine. Smooth, actually.

During the commercial breaks, he became himself again. He stared off into space, flipped blankly through his cards, and muttered "shit"—pronounced "shee-it"—over and over, like a tic. Jackson closed the show with his trademark slogan: "Keep hope alive."

For viewers, I don't think it was a very exciting half hour. For me, it was a profound education. Jesse Jackson was a lot phonier than I'd even imagined.

Looking back, I think I judged Jackson too harshly. Yes, he was and is a phony, world-class by any definition. But television exacerbated his phoniness. The producers catered to his laziness by doing his work for him. The star treatment inflamed his natural cynicism and arrogance. The medium itself made him more pompous than he already was. TV was bad for Jesse Jackson's soul.

And he's not alone. Television magnifies almost everything about a person, from the pimples on his nose to his temper. I once knew a talk show host who insisted, above all else, that every other person on the set appear shorter than him. He wasn't a tall man, so this required the producers to lower everyone else's chair. It was obvious to all present what was going on, and it was really embarrassing. I used to wonder: Does he attempt this in restaurants?

Of course he doesn't, and not just because restaurants don't have adjustable chairs. It was being on television that made him feel tiny. Already uncomfortable with his height, he grew intensely insecure the moment he stepped onto a set. You can see what could happen to you after years of having your native traits amplified by television. You could become a caricature of yourself.

Chris Matthews struggles with this. On *Hardball,* his nightly MSNBC show, Matthews is famously manic. He talks at the speed of an auctioneer. He switches topics in midsentence. He has no attention span, interrupting anyone who hasn't made a stunning point or an explosive allegation within four seconds. Sometimes he'll interrupt anyway, just to get back to talking.

The amazing thing is, this is not an act. Off the air, Matthews is almost exactly the same way. You have to speak in

New York Post headlines or he can't hear you. A typical green-room exchange with Matthews might go something like this:

YOU: Hey, Chris, are there any coffee cups in here?

MATTHEWS: That's what Adlai Stevenson said at the Chicago convention in 'fifty-two—"If this cup may not pass from me, except that I drink it, Thy will be done." Like he's Jesus. What is it with politicians? They all think they're God. George Burns played God, but at least he knew it was only a role. The guy lived to be like, a hundred. I wouldn't want to hang around that long. Every life has three acts, like a play. Intermission is the part where—

YOU: Chris. Chris. Cups?

MATTHEWS: You got to wear one when you play hockey. Tip O'Neill used to say that's what happened to Dukakis. Jerry Ford played football without a helmet; Mike Dukakis played hockey without a cup. They don't play hockey in L.A. I was there last month. Got a cameo in the new Eminem movie . . .

There's a certain charm in this. The free association, the speed-freak delivery—it's fun to listen to. In order to talk like this, you have to believe that what you have to say is incredibly interesting, that all of your thoughts are worth sharing with other people at all times. This is a risky assumption.

It's one that all talk show hosts seem to make after a while. A couple of years ago, I wound up sitting across from John McLaughlin and his wife on the train from New York to

Washington. McLaughlin is a former Catholic priest who, in the early 1980s, created *The McLaughlin Group,* one of the longest-running and most successful political debate shows on television. He was reading the *New York Times* when I got on the train. He looked up and saw me. "Have you seen this story? It's remarkable." McLaughlin spoke in his normal voice, which is also his TV voice and therefore recognizable to millions. And he spoke very loudly, as he always does. The car was packed. I'm certain every single person was listening.

The story was about pornography. The state of Utah, the *Times* had discovered, is a hotbed of porn. Despite their strait-laced reputation, Utah residents love dirty movies. Apparently, they watch an unusually large number of them. It was an interesting piece, if not all that surprising.

But for McLaughlin, the *Times* account was merely a starting point for more general ruminations on pornography: the increasing availability of adult videos, their rising quality, the merits of DirecTV porn versus EchoStar porn versus the Hot Network. He knew quite a lot about it. So did the entire train by the end of the lecture.

I've never had a more enjoyable trip to Washington, though I wondered what everyone else in the car thought. I doubt McLaughlin cared. I'm not sure he even realized there were other people around.

McLaughlin isn't famous for his sensitivity, but that's not why he felt comfortable talking about pornography in an enclosed space full of strangers. He felt comfortable because he's a veteran talk show host. After years of performing, you tend to become oblivious to your audience. You lose track of what you're not supposed to say out loud.

Not to mention what you're not supposed to do. One night I was having dinner in Washington with a friend of mine who hosts a television show. Two women in a nearby booth asked if we'd mind if they smoked. Of course not, we said. On our way out, my friend walked over to introduce himself. One of the women had just gotten her dessert, an elaborate-looking piece of cheesecake. As he talked, my friend dug his fingers into it, prying off the walnuts and popping them into his mouth. Soon his hand was covered with frosting, which he licked off with long, catlike tongue strokes.

The women were speechless. They were tourists, and clearly unacquainted with Washington table manners. More remarkable was my friend, who seemed completely oblivious both to what he was doing and to the women's reaction. I guess it all seemed normal to him.

This is the curse of the professional extrovert. If you're not careful, you can permanently lose all critical distance from yourself. One morning you wake up, and you're living in your own irony-free world. This, sadly, is what has happened to Bill O'Reilly, the host of Fox's *O'Reilly Factor,* the highest-rated show in cable news.

Critics claim that O'Reilly is popular because he panders to the reactionary opinions of his audience. This is a shallow critique. O'Reilly understands television better than almost anyone working in it. He's a skillful debater. His delivery is perfect. He expresses himself with absolute clarity. He is a master of the medium.

And, like everyone in TV, he has a shtick. O'Reilly is Everyman—the faithful but slightly lapsed Catholic son of the working class who knows slick, eastern Establishment BS when he sees it. A guy who tells the truth and demands that others do the same. A man who won't be pushed around or take maybe for an answer. A populist, basically, but a modern one. Biased, not bigoted. Above all, a person who is committed to fairness and the idea of meritocracy.

It works. But there's a price. O'Reilly's success is built on the perception that he really is who he claims to be. If he ever gets caught out of character, it's over. If someday he punches out a flight attendant on the Concorde for bringing him a glass of warm champagne, the whole franchise will come tumbling down. He'll make the whatever-happened-to . . . ? list quicker than you can say "Morton Downey Jr."

I don't think it will happen. Like everybody, O'Reilly is more complicated than his image. (He went to Harvard for graduate school, after all, not Holy Cross or SUNY Purchase.) But he is becoming less complicated and more like the person he depicts on TV. You expect O'Reilly to play the part of a blustery tough guy on his show. It's disconcerting to think he does it off the air. But, as anyone who works at the Fox News Channel in New York can tell you, he does. Maybe he can't help it anymore.

I once sat with O'Reilly on a panel in Washington. The discussion topic was "The Press in Wartime," and someone asked O'Reilly what he thought of the media coverage of the fighting in Afghanistan. Rather than simply answer the question, O'Reilly began by trying to establish his own bona fides as a war correspondent. "I've covered wars, okay? I've been there. The Falklands, Northern Ireland, the Middle East. I've almost been killed three times, okay?"

O'Reilly said this to a group that included experienced journalists, some of whom had covered genuinely dangerous wars, not the Falklands, not Belfast, not stand-ups from the balcony of the Tel Aviv Hilton. Real war correspondents have one of the riskiest jobs in the world; in almost every war, they're killed at a much higher rate than soldiers. O'Reilly had just patronized them in the most ludicrous possible way. It was a little like bragging about your National Guard service to a room full of Navy SEALs.

No one called him on it. I bet no one ever does. I imagine it's been years since anyone he works with has told O'Reilly to stop talking about himself so goddamn much, and to quit referring to himself in the third person as "The Big Guy." That simply never happens to O'Reilly anymore. In Bill O'Reilly's world, there are only flatterers.

I know how network handlers talk to O'Reilly because I've been talked to the same way myself, and my ratings aren't nearly as good: "You're a superstar. No, you really are. I'm not just saying it. You're a superstar. You. Are. A. Superstar. I mean that." And it gets more sugary from there.

Which is not to knock flattery. I spent an entire summer being addressed as "Asshole" by the manager of the Exxon station I worked at, so I never sniff at compliments. But you can't believe them. You become unbearable if you do.

The Electrical College

✳ ✳ ✳

Every talk show needs guests. Which means that no talk show would exist without publicity hounds. If you watch cable news, you know who they are, because they're always on the tube. Robert Wexler. Bob Barr. Julian Epstein. Gloria Allred. Bookers have their own name for ever-ready guests like these: "easy turns." An easy turn is someone who will leave his son's sixth birthday party to make it to the studio in time to get barked at for eight minutes on cable. We love easy turns. They help us when we're desperate.

And, of course, they love us. Most of them have something to sell: a book, a radio show, a law practice, a political career. We give them publicity. They give us what they know. It's a transaction. It may be vulgar, but it's not weird.

Weird is when they're not selling anything. These are the guests that even the bookers have contempt for, the ones who will blow off their six-year-olds for no other reason than that they like being on television. Adore it. Love it. Live for it. People like Jerry Falwell.

Falwell's critics describe him as intolerant. They obviously haven't talked to him about television. When Falwell talks about people he appears with on the talk show circuit, he's all love and forgiveness. I know this because I once spent a day with Falwell, doing research for a magazine piece on the political influence of Christian conservatives. I never finished the story, partly because Falwell was no help at all. He was friendly enough, and chatty. But he didn't seem interested in talking about politics, or religion. He wanted to talk about television.

The two of us spent the morning touring his church, Thomas Road Baptist, where he has served as pastor since 1956. Falwell has preached thousands of sermons from the pulpit, but in the hours we spent together, he hardly mentioned God. Instead, he pointed enthusiastically to the seven television cameras he had installed around the church to film his weekly program, the *Old Time Gospel Hour*. He showed me the church's control room, the enormous soundboard, its videotape archive, and editing booths. On the way out, we passed Falwell's private study. Hanging on the wall outside, positioned at eye level, was a photograph of Falwell with his arm around Bill Maher. Both were grinning. "I do *Politically Incorrect* about four or five times a year," Falwell said. "Bill Maher is very fair."

Bill Maher is also vehemently and loudly opposed to almost everything Jerry Falwell ostensibly stands for and believes in. Falwell didn't seem to mind. Maher is a television friend, the best kind. As is Larry King, who, Falwell gushed, is "superbright. Larry has improved with every day. You think some of these guys are just beyond improvement. But Larry gets better all the time. He has a great capacity to learn and to grow. And he's a friend."

Alan Dershowitz, meanwhile, is not the most annoying person in modern history, at least according to Falwell. He may seem like a grating, unbearable blowhard, but if you know him like Falwell does, from the fraternity of the greenroom, you'll realize Dershowitz is "an excellent, excellent lawyer," worthy of the deepest respect. "I wouldn't consider him a media person," Falwell explained in what must rank among the least true sentences ever uttered.

As for Geraldo Rivera, well, said Falwell with a self-satisfied chuckle, "Geraldo and I are *very* good friends. I just think he's a brilliant fellow." Indeed, almost a blood brother. "There's not much that I could ask him or he could ask me to do that one of us wouldn't do for the other one," Falwell said. Rivera told me later that he and Falwell had never actually met.

There was a time when Falwell saw television primarily as a tool for evangelism—he told one biographer in the early 1980s that he would never make a public appearance without preaching the Gospel—but that was several 24-hour news networks ago. These days Falwell sounds more like a television producer than a televangelist. He uses insider technical terms like "bump" and "tight shot" and "voice-over." He refers to the satellite that carries his appearances as "the bird." He casually mentions the "three or four" specialists he has on staff "who are trained at all times to handle makeup."

And, of course, he talks—and talks and talks—about the shows he has appeared on. "I guess there's some I haven't done, but I can't think of them," he told me. "I do *Larry King* quite often. I do *Nightline*—I did *Nightline* eleven times in one year. I do *Hardball*. I do a lot of the CNN news shows. I do all the network news shows on a regular basis. Six weeks ago, I did the ABC, CBS, and NBC morning news shows the same day."

Falwell didn't mention that, in order to make it on all three shows, he had to agree to discuss whether certain cartoon characters might be gay. ("How are you on the issue of Barney?" asked ABC's Charles Gibson in a representative question.) Not that it seemed to matter to Falwell. It's good enough that he was on.

For Falwell, appearing on television is an intrinsically positive event, a self-justifying act, an end in itself. Jerry Falwell does TV because he believes it is Good. In a theological sense.

I remember how disappointed I was when I figured this out. I'd gone to the interview assuming Falwell would live up to his reputation as an uncompromising right-wing ideologue. Instead, he was just another publicity hound. And he wasn't even that amusing.

If you're going to be shallow, I've always thought, you'd better be amusing. One night at dinner I sat next to a well-known southern senator who is both. We were seated at a large round table, with his wife directly across the way on the other side of the floral arrangement. About five glasses of wine into the meal, the senator, apropos of nothing, began to tell me about his new scheduler, a "hot little girl from Texas. And I mean *hot*." He then indicated—saying it without saying it, but clearly saying it—that he was sleeping with her. I was amazed.

Later that week I happened to run into the same senator's chief political consultant. Bragging about your extramarital sexual conquests to a journalist you don't know very well, while seated eight feet from your wife, struck me as a pretty rash thing to do, so I told the consultant about it. He smiled. "That's a riot," he said. "And sad, too. He had prostate surgery a couple of years ago. He hasn't gotten it up since. He's not sleeping with anybody. I think he just says things like that to make himself feel better."

To this day, I don't know who was lying, the senator or his consultant. One of them is a talented BS artist. I respect that.

There's no BS artist whose work I respected more than the late M. Larry Lawrence. He was a giant in his field, the Michelangelo of untruth. Lawrence was the San Diego hotel owner appointed by President Clinton to be U.S. ambassador to Switzerland. Shortly after he died, Lawrence was discovered to have made up details about his war record. A minor scandal ensued, and his body was disinterred from Arlington National Cemetery. That's what most people remember.

What they forget is the thrilling audacity of his lies. In November 1993, during a Senate Foreign Relations Committee hearing, Lawrence reminisced about his wartime exploits in the U.S. Merchant Marine. Keep in mind that the future ambassador to Switzerland spoke these words, every one of them untrue, with a straight face into a microphone before a room full of U.S. senators:

> I was eighteen years old and I was on board the SS *Horace Bushnell* in a convoy to Murmansk, which was an all-volunteer run known as the "Suicide Mission." We were torpedoed fifteen miles off Murmansk. I was just coming out of the hole, and everybody down below was killed.

I was thrown clear. I am told—I have no memory of what happened—that thereafter I suffered a serious concussion and was taken in a coma, subsequently, after going in the water, to Murmansk, then Scotland, and back to New York and home. It is something I do not particularly relish remembering for the record, Senator. You know. You were there. I told them to mail me the medal, but my wife insisted that we have the ceremony.

Silence fell on the hearing room as Lawrence revealed the purpose of the Suicide Mission. "We were delivering food and ammunition," he explained. "That, of course, is what caused the main explosion, as the torpedo struck the ammunition."

Several senators were clearly impressed. Yet even this wasn't the whole story. Ever the bashful man of valor, Lawrence had left out his own glorious role, the part about how, while floating gravely wounded in ice-crusted Arctic waters, he had ignored his injuries to save the lives of fellow sailors. Senator Diane Feinstein, reading from a crib sheet Lawrence himself had helped prepare, filled in the blanks. "He was able to rescue others," she said. "He was deemed a hero."

Four years later, of course, he was deemed a liar. None of it happened. Once Lawrence's hoax was exposed, the White House scrambled to explain how such a whopper could have slipped through the ambassador's background check. As one Clinton official told the *Washington Post,* "Because we were able to go to friends, business associates, an array of people who gave us a glowing recommendation, it mitigated against having to go back and chase ghost records of Merchant Marine service." There was no reason to check the war story, the official explained, because an extensive investigation into Lawrence's past had yielded no "derogatory information."

It's not clear which "array of people" State Department investigators spoke to about Lawrence (who, just for starters, had more than two dozen cases pending against him in federal tax court at the time he was nominated). It is clear they didn't talk to many people in San Diego, where Lawrence lived and did business. Soon after the Merchant Marine story broke, the *San Diego Union-Tribune* sent two reporters to get reaction from people who knew Lawrence well. The reporters returned a few hours later with more derogatory information about Larry Lawrence than State Department sleuths had managed to gather in months.

"I wouldn't take his word for anything," a longtime senior vice president of Lawrence's Hotel del Coronado told the newspaper. "He had a terrible, terrible case of vanity," said one of his pallbearers. According to Lucy Goldman, described as a close friend and former neighbor, Lawrence had a habit of dropping "little bombshells" during conversation. "I remember once we went to a rodeo together," Goldman recalled, "and Larry was sitting next to me and said, 'Do you know I used to do this in Arizona?'"

Lawrence also claimed that he used to play professional football. He told other friends that he "went to the University of Chicago for law." In fact, Lawrence, who was not a lawyer, attended Wilbur Wright Junior College. He bragged on his résumé about being the "vice chair" of the "Nobel Peace Prize Nominating Commission." Strictly speaking, there is no such thing.

Yes, lies like these are offensive, maybe even evil. But there's a kind of artistry to what Larry Lawrence did. He didn't just tell lies. He spun them out of pure air and wove them into intricate tapestries of untruth. He was a craftsman working in the medium of duplicity. True BS artisans like Larry Lawrence are a vanishing breed.

One of the last I encountered was Steve Glass. Glass, you may remember, was expelled from journalism when it was discovered he had made up whole magazine articles and everything in them: people, quotes, crimes, companies, trends, imaginary pieces of legislation pending before Congress. You name it, Glass concocted it. In a single story on global climate change, he invented at least three different environmental organizations and their spokesmen, even quoted from their nonexistent press releases. Glass's facts were brazenly, verifiably, obviously false, yet he continued to fool editors at places like *Harper's*, the *New Republic*, and *Rolling Stone*.

Not to mention me. Glass and I were friends. We ate lunch together once or twice a month, usually on an expense account supplied by whatever magazine he was on assignment for. Glass always had amazing stories, about the stockbroker he interviewed who worshiped at a shrine dedicated to Alan Greenspan, or the months he spent working as a telephone psychic. Over one lunch, Glass told me about his plan to appear on the *Jerry Springer Show*. He'd convinced the producers that he was part of a violent and bizarre love triangle and wanted to talk about it on the air. It was a hoax, he said, but they believed it.

Glass's brief but remarkable career in journalism came to a fittingly dramatic end one day in the spring of 1998. Glass had written a story for the *New Republic* about a teenage computer hacker named Ian Restil. Though only fifteen, Restil was able to hack into the innermost databases of a high-tech corporation called Jukt Micronics and post photographs of nude women on its Web site. Executives at Jukt were so impressed by Restil's skill, Glass wrote, that they offered him a job. Glass recorded what he described as the boy's contract demands: "I want more money. I want a Miata. I want a trip to Disney World. I want X-Man comic number one. I want a lifetime subscription to *Playboy,* and throw in *Penthouse.* Show me the money! Show me the money!"

Even by Glass's standards the story was a bit much. One suspicious reader, who happened to work at an on-line business publication, attempted to locate Jukt Micronics. Unable to find any mention of the company, he called the *New Republic.* Glass was cornered. But he didn't give up. Instead, he furiously dug deeper. Glass produced a phone number for Jukt's headquarters (in fact, the voice mail of his younger brother's cell phone), as well as the address of the nonexistent company's Web site, on which he had posted criticism of his own article.

Clever as it was, it only delayed the inevitable. Within days, Glass was exposed in the pages of the *Washington Post.* He was fired from the *New Republic,* as well as from his many other journalism jobs. He has since left Washington and become a lawyer (and, for a brief time in 2003, a failed novelist). I didn't realize it at the time, but his departure marked the end of an era. Increasingly, high-end frauds like Glass and Larry Lawrence have been replaced by brute liars, demagogues who substitute aggression for finesse and creativity. Guys like Jesse Jackson.

Like Glass and Lawrence, Jackson has been repeatedly exposed in public as dishonest. But unlike them, he has not had the decency to fade from public view. Though he no longer hosts his own show, Jackson lives on in television as a constantly recurring guest. All of his on-air experience hasn't made Jackson more appealing. He has no obvious sense of humor, he tends to give sermons rather than answers, and he can be very hard to understand. But his years on the talk show circuit have done one thing for him: They've made Jackson the master of the televised lie.

Jesse Jackson understands one of the central facts about live television: It's very difficult to cross-examine someone on the air effectively, particularly someone who speaks quickly and in a disjointed way. If a guest makes an unsubstantiated allegation on a TV show, the host can call him on it. If the guest makes ten of them in sixty seconds, there's not much the host can do. The words fly out, hang in the air for a moment, then disappear. There isn't time to catch and challenge each one.

I've had the experience with Jackson countless times, but one particularly bewildering exchange stands out in my mind. It was midway through the Florida recount of 2000 when Jackson came on *The Spin Room*. I asked him a fairly simple question. He exploded like a cluster bomb of nonsense. Halfway through his first response, he accused George W. Bush of mocking "Holocaust survivors" and "Haitian immigrants." Then he charged unspecified Republican officials in Florida with "corruption" and other "crimes punishable by jail sentences."

And then Jackson talked about himself: "I seek to empower people. I seek to enfranchise people. I seek to build coalitions. So fighting for racial justice and fighting for fairness and democracy is my way of offering my service to America. . . ." He went on. But I was having trouble following it. I was still wondering about the Holocaust survivors. Bush mocked them?

I never caught up with Jesse Jackson. He moved too fast, blowing right through conventional barriers of logic and grammar. By the time he delivered his final assessment of the election, I was miles behind. "My concern," Jackson concluded, is

"Duvall County, where 27,000 ballots were thrown away, perhaps 16,000 black, because the wards they were in, that when Congresswoman Brown was trying to negotiate because there were some complaints, negotiating about 500 ballots. But they found it at 11:00 on the third night. That's 72 hours after you could no longer protest. It was 27,000, not 500. And that was the night before Veteran's Day. So they could not protest a contest until the sixth day. That's an intentionality. Does it matter that 27,000 voters in Jacksonville are disenfranchised? Does it matter that 33,000 Americans in West Palm Beach got a ballot, a sample ballot, that was different than the real ballot? They said—does that matter?"

It didn't matter to me. All that mattered to me was getting this guy off the air. I got into bed that night still brooding about the show. The more I thought about Jackson, the madder I got, both at him and at myself. I couldn't believe I let him ramble on like that on the air. Not that I had much choice. It would have taken hours to unravel what he was saying, much less rebut it. I don't think I'll ever understand the part about Veteran's Day.

It's almost impossible to argue with people who will say anything, though some attempts are more pleasant than others. I've debated Al Sharpton as many times as I have Jesse Jackson and never come away irritated. Sharpton often seems to be impersonating Jackson, after whom he has self-consciously modeled his career. But the similarities are mostly cosmetic. Sharpton is smarter, funnier, and much less self-righteous. As Roger Stone once put it after dealing with both of them during his years as a political consultant in New York, "Al and Jesse both shake you down, but Jesse makes you pray before you give him the money." Al just grins as you fork over the bills.

Nothing rattles Al Sharpton. I learned this for certain one night on *Crossfire* in the summer of 2002 when I first saw a copy of the Sharpton drug tape. Shot by federal narcotics agents more than a decade before, the grainy Abscam-like footage showed Sharpton sitting in a room with an undercover cop. The reverend was dressed in a leather jacket and a cowboy hat. He had his boots propped on the desk and a cigar in his mouth. He and the under-cover cop were talking about kilos of cocaine. The effect was completely damning. If the average person was caught looking like Al Sharpton looked in the tape, he'd leave the country, or do the honorable thing and kill himself. The average person couldn't handle it.

Al Sharpton is not the average person. We rolled the tape. Sharpton didn't even wince. Instead, he immediately demanded to see "the rest of the tapes." For a second, this caught me off guard; I wasn't aware there *were* other tapes. Sharpton sensed my confusion and pushed forward. "What we're doing tomorrow," he said, his voice rising with outrage, "is filing a lawsuit. We are ask-ing for the Freedom of Information Act. Let's release all the tapes. And I'm going to ask all presidential candidates, including Presi-dent Bush, let's all say to the government: Release the tapes!"

Do "the rest of the tapes" even exist? I still don't know. Sharpton never explained what might be on them, who might have them, or what they might have to do with the tape we'd just shown. But it didn't matter. He had successfully changed the subject from his own, obviously shady behavior to the behavior of the government. In effect, he changed the topic of the show. We were no longer talking about Al Sharpton's brush with fed-eral narcotics agents. We were talking about a sinister attempt by certain Powerful Figures to perpetrate a diabolical cover-up—a conspiracy, really, to undermine legitimate black leadership in this country and, by extension, the Voting Rights Act itself. Or at least that's what Sharpton was talking about.

On one level, I was frustrated. On another, I was impressed. With Sharpton, at least you know you're being bamboozled.

Not so with Congressman Chris Shays. Shays is a wily guy, but he doesn't look it. Mild-mannered and polite, a Christian Scientist who doesn't drink coffee or raise his voice, the Connecticut Republican is the first person you'd ask to hold your wallet. He has that look: clean, like he takes a dozen showers a day and rolls in talcum powder after every one. Chris Shays doesn't give off shifty vibes.

Never judge a congressman by his cover. On the night of the 2002 campaign finance reform vote in the House, I interviewed Shays on *Crossfire*. My first question was the obvious one: If soft money is so terrible—and your bill is based on the premise that it is—then why not ban it immediately? Why does your legislation allow soft money in this November's midterm elections?

It's a hard question to answer, and not surprisingly, Shays didn't. The remarkable part was how he evaded it. "You know, we have feedback," he said. "I can hardly hear you." And with that, he removed his earpiece, leaving me, in a studio across town, unable to ask him another question or force him to answer the first one. Freed from the bothersome give-and-take of an interview, he began his speech: "I can't hear you, but the bottom line is, we are looking to ban corporate treasury money and union dues money, enforcing the 1907 law, the 1947 law, and then enforce the 1974 law that says: no large contributions. And that's what we're attempting to do."

The other guest, a fellow congressman who was sitting next to Shays, looked confused. His earpiece wasn't giving him trouble. He could hear everything I said. And so, I suspect, could

Shays. I checked later: His audio connection worked. The "feedback" wasn't caused by technical problems.

Pretty crafty. And doubly so, given Shays's reputation. You'd never suspect him of doing something like that. He's the shop-lifting nun.

The next morning, the *Washington Post* was none the wiser. A fawning profile described Shays as a man with "the avuncular bearing of a beloved high school teacher—a mentor who, in retrospect, might seem a little naive." Far from a calculating political operative, Shays, readers learned, is "slightly goofy, a man prone to giving surprise noogies on the House floor, hug-ging his fellow members, mussing their hair and breaking spas-modically into pitched giggles."

Shays did his best to remain in character. At sunup, he told the *Post,* he jogs to one of Washington's many memorials, med-itating on the life of the statesman remembered there. The week of the vote on campaign finance reform, Shays stopped at the Lincoln Memorial. There, at the nation's temple to fairness and political courage, "he read aloud from the Gettysburg Address in the dawn solitude." In case you missed the point, the headline summed it up: "The GOP's Reluctant Rebel."

Fairly amusing—and completely, totally wrong. In fact, there has never been anything reluctant about Shays's rebellions. In 1998, he was one of five House Republicans to vote against every article of Clinton's impeachment. By itself, this is not an especially telling fact. Shays is from a swing district that generally supported Clinton. It was his flamboyant media-mongering that set Shays apart from less savvy moderates.

Early in the Lewinsky scandal, Shays announced that he planned to vote against impeachment. Then, days before the vote, he announced he was reconsidering. There's nothing more newsworthy than a vote in play, and Shays leveraged his. He invited reporters to accompany him as he staged one-on-one encounter groups with his constituents to talk about impeachment. ("'What's been on your mind?' Shays asks gently. 'You want to tell me how you feel?'") He moderated a televised town hall meeting in his district. More than 2,000 people came, including Paul Newman. The following day, he requested, and got, a meeting with Clinton at the White House.

Shays quickly became famous, though he was careful never to seem pleased about it. He continued to play the role of the sensitive, world-averse artiste trapped in the body of a Connecticut congressman. He cried in public and boasted about it later. Conservatives were infuriated. Columnist Ann Coulter (who for a time talked about challenging him in the primary) implied that Shays was gay.

It was a classic case of taking Chris Shays too seriously. It's not easy being a professional reformer in Washington, a city that isn't very corrupt and therefore not in desperate need of reform. To do it, you need a shtick. Shays has picked the "Tormented Conscience of a Nation" routine. It's the least appealing of all options.

And there are options, like Marty Meehan, the Democratic cosponsor of Shays's bill. Meehan has all the florid charm of the straightforward stereotype he is, the Irish Catholic sports fan beer drinker from Mill Town, Massachusetts. (Meehan named his son Bobby, after RFK.) With Meehan, you can safely assume he's found some angle in campaign finance reform. When he preens, it sounds less like self-righteousness than like someone doing an imitation of it. It's entertaining.

But for pure entertainment value, no one beats Senator John McCain. McCain often invokes Teddy Roosevelt when he talks about campaign finance reform, and in at least one sense the comparison is fair. Like Roosevelt, McCain is drawn to Reform not by the reforms themselves, but by what they represent. For McCain, campaign finance reform isn't an end but a metaphor: the struggle of the little guy against the big guy, the Special Interests versus the People, the defenseless versus the bully. Trap McCain in a conversation about the actual details of campaign finance reform and he soon loses focus. He's bored by it.

But he puts on an impressive show. McCain understands that if you're going to play the reformer, sad-eyed disapproval won't do. You've got to pick up the hatchet. McCain does a terrific Carry Nation impression. It's effective because on some level it's real. McCain has a genuinely bad temper. He is a genuinely tough guy.

During his first run for office, McCain learned that one of his opponents had tracked down his first wife, looking for dirt. According to a political consultant who worked for him at the time, McCain cornered the man at the next candidate's forum. "I want you to know," McCain said, "that, campaign aside, politics aside, you ever do anything like that again—anything against a person in my family—and I will personally beat the shit out of you."

It's impossible to imagine Chris Shays threatening to personally beat the shit out of anyone. But it would be a lot easier to like him if he did.

Almost no one in Washington physically threatens anyone anymore. In general, the city has become a hotbed of politeness. You rarely see politicians yell or point fingers or use vulgar language. Almost everyone in Congress these days has good manners, at least in public. In some ways, this is a positive trend. But as a talk show host, I'm bothered by it. Politics deserves more color. The legislative process needs more people like Don Young.

Young, the Republican congressman from Alaska, once used a walrus penis bone as a prop during a congressional hearing. As Mollie Beatty, then the director of the federal Fish and Wildlife Service, spoke about the need to protect endangered species from hunting, Young angrily slapped the eighteen-inch bone against his hand.

Not long after that, Young, a former trapper, returned to Fairbanks, where he gave a speech at a local high school. Young's talk included a rant about the evils of federally funded art, especially the kind that includes "photographs of people doing offensive things." What kinds of things? a student wondered. "Butt-fucking," replied the congressman. "You think that's art?"

I've never asked Senator Ernest Hollings what he thinks of Robert Mapplethorpe, but I'm confident he could improve on Young's answer. Hollings, a Democrat who arrived in the Senate during the Kennedy Administration, is legendary for his Tourette's-like inability to control the unpleasant comments that flow from his mouth. He may be the nastiest politician in Washington.

During a 1984 forum for Democratic presidential hopefuls in New Hampshire, Hollings, on live television, mocked former Florida governor Reubin Askew's facial twitch. "You've got a tic in your ear, too," he snapped. During a newspaper interview in the fall of 1992, he predicted that Strom Thurmond would never leave the Senate while still breathing. Without his job in Washington, Hollings explained, Thurmond wouldn't "have a home, a hometown, and would quickly discover he doesn't have any real friends." Already, Hollings pointed out, his wife "Nancy left him."

Senile or not, Thurmond was still a hero in South Carolina, and Hollings's opponent that year, former Republican congressman Tommy Hartnett, tried to use Hollings's words against him. "I believe you owe Senator Thurmond an apology," Hartnett said during a debate. "And I'm asking you to apologize." Hollings didn't even consider it. "You're full of prunes," he said.

By Hollings's standards, this was restraint. When the Japanese premier described American workers as "illiterate and lazy," Hollings gave a speech in which he proposed responding with a cartoon: "You should draw a mushroom cloud and put underneath it, 'Made in America by lazy and illiterate Americans and tested in Japan.'"

During a Senate debate over school prayer, Hollings—whose description of Senator Lloyd Bentsen as "the senator from Texaco" was already notorious—described Howard Metzenbaum of Ohio as "the senator from B'nai B'rith." The phrase was later removed from the record, but reporters had heard it. Hollings was forced to apologize. "I was talking intentionally, in the spirit of levity that we had on the floor at the time," he explained.

Fellow senators were familiar with the Hollings brand of levity. In the summer of 1989, he infuriated his colleagues during Senator John Tower's confirmation hearings by quoting from a confidential FBI report that described Tower's alleged drinking problem. Over loud objections, Hollings repeatedly referred to Tower as "Mr. Alcoholic Abuser": "Put in Mr. Alcoholic Abuser as Secretary of Defense? Man, what you talkin' about in this body?"

Outbursts like these have worried Hollings's friends for years. His staff does its best to keep the senator away from chance encounters with journalists. It doesn't always work. Hollings once explained to a television crew how foreign imports were taking minimum-wage jobs away from South Carolina's "darkies." Another time, he told a reporter that he was looking forward to a trip to Switzerland because "everybody likes to go to Geneva. I used to do it for the Law of the Sea conferences and you'd find these potentates from down in Africa, you know. Rather than eating each other, they'd just come up and get a good square meal in Geneva."

"This man is mentally sick," observed the head of the South Carolina NAACP after Hollings's cannibalism interview. "He has to have something wrong in his head to keep making these kinds of comments." Hollings didn't seem to care. He had already described the NAACP as a "lynch mob."

Had Hollings been a Republican, there's little doubt he would have received the Trent Lott treatment. Jesse Jackson would have held a press conference on his front lawn. But Hollings isn't a Republican, and for that reason he has continued to win the vast majority of the state's black vote.

Republicans in South Carolina knew they couldn't do anything about Hollings's black support, but in 1998 they decided they could defeat him with his own bad manners. The challenger that year was Bob Inglis, a friendly but hapless conservative from upstate. Inglis drafted what he called a "Contract for a Courteous Campaign," then pushed Hollings to sign it. Essentially a written promise not to engage in negative campaigning, the document contained, among other gimmicks, a requirement that each candidate give the other rebuttal time at press conferences.

The very idea of such a contract sent Hollings into a fury. Inglis, he told reporters, was "an oozing and goozing" "little choirboy." "Everybody's rude and he wants to be nice. He's a goddamned skunk" who, Hollings said, can "kiss my fanny." Hollings went on to denounce "all this ying-yow about courtesy" as "nonsense" and "trickery." "I've been elected six times," he said. "I've gotten along with all my candidates before and didn't have to get a contract."

Contract or not, it wasn't clear that Hollings could stop being nasty even if he wanted to. After one particularly acrimonious debate with Inglis, a reporter approached Hollings for comment. You said some tough things out there about Congressman Inglis, the reporter said, but politics aside, you like and respect him personally, don't you? "Not at all," replied Hollings, totally unrepentant. "I can tell you that right here and now."

In the end, voters chose Hollings by a wide margin. And it's not hard to see why. Despite everything, he's a pretty appealing ambassador for their state. He's a terrific television guest. Consider an appearance he made on the old Sunday morning David Brinkley show on ABC. Hollings went on at some length in his Foghorn Leghorn low-country accent expounding on the importance of maintaining trade barriers against low-quality, probably disease- and vermin-ridden foreign textiles. Sam Donaldson let Hollings ramble, then sprung the trap.

"Senator," Donaldson asked, "you're from the great textile-producing state of South Carolina. Is it true you have a Korean tailor?"

Hollings pulled back his lapel, glanced at the tag, then calmly turned to Donaldson. "I bought it the same place," he said, "where you got that wig, Sam."

It was perhaps the most awkward moment in the history of network television, and in its own way, a triumph. Hollings may have bad manners, but at least he's fun to watch.

Representative Barney Frank of Massachusetts, by contrast, defies all probability by being even more unpleasant in person than he is on television. I once had the unhappy experience of sitting next to Frank for more than an hour on a set. During the first commercial break, the producer, a meek blonde woman of about twenty-five, came out to adjust the back of Frank's blazer, which had bunched up around his neck. "Congressman," she said sweetly, leaning forward, "do you mind if I just—"

"Hey," he growled, pushing her back. "I'm not some Hollywood airhead. I'm not here to look good. I'm here to talk about substance. Or is that against the rules now?" The woman was confused. "I'm sorry, Congressman," she said. "But your coat—" Frank cut her off and launched into a lecture about how what his coat looked like didn't matter, and if she would just stop pestering him about frivolous matters of appearance maybe we could get to the issues, start solving the problems that ordinary Americans really care about. The producer looked as if she was about to cry.

It was pure viciousness. I made a mental note to devote the rest of my life to subverting Frank's career. During the next break I did my best to torment him. For a guy who doesn't care what he looks like, I said, you sure have on a lot of makeup. Frank glared at me, then went back to chewing his fingernails, one of which was already bloody.

It was clear he didn't plan to respond, so I pushed him: Hey, Barney, what's the deal with the makeup? Looks pretty Hollywood. "I didn't want to make a fuss," he mumbled, "so I just let them put it on." Right, I said, chuckling. At the end of the show, just before he stormed off the set, Frank glanced up from his fingernails and gave me a murderous look. "I think you're filled with hatred," he hissed.

If you live in Washington, you've probably heard people say what a witty guy Barney Frank is. And he may be, by the low standards of the Democratic party. This is a shame, as well as a break with history.

Liberals used to be funny. They edited magazines like *National Lampoon*. They had a claim on cool. Then something happened. They became sour and earnest and neurotic about secondhand smoke. The Democratic party became the party of the uptight establishment, the that's-not-funny-young-man party, the party of no fun. *National Lampoon* folded. At least one of its editors became a conservative and started writing for the *American Spectator*.

If you began reading the *American Spectator* in the mid-1990s, you probably remember it for obsessive, slightly kooky (sometimes very kooky) investigative journalism that wasn't all that interesting unless you hated Bill Clinton for a living. But before Clinton, believe it or not, it was a very funny magazine.

In the summer of 1989, the *Spectator* published an article titled "A Call for a New McCarthyism" by P. J. O'Rourke, late of *National Lampoon*. O'Rourke opened the piece by conceding that the liberals were absolutely right: The Reagan years had in fact been a replay of the darkest days of the 1950s. "Indeed," he wrote, "we are experiencing anew many of the pleasures and benefits of that excellent decade: a salubrious prudery, a sensible avariciousness, a healthy dose of social conformity, a much-needed narrowing of the minds, and a return to common-sense American political troglodytism."

According to O'Rourke, the only thing missing from the '80s was a good old-fashioned witch hunt. So he started one: "The fun part of McCarthyism is, as it always was, making out the enemies list." O'Rourke's list included "fuzzy-minded one-worlders, pasty-faced peace creeps, and bleeding-heart bed-wetters" like Sting and Amy Carter.

O'Rourke wrote the piece for the same reason Fox News Channel calls itself "Fair and Balanced": to drive liberals crazy. It worked. Years later, when the essay was expanded into a book, an outraged reviewer at *Library Journal* huffed that O'Rourke was trying to revive "the ghosts of Joe McCarthy and Richard Nixon."

Bait taken.

It's both the job and the privilege of a political party to glee-fully torment its opponents. Democrats seem to have forgotten this. Ever read the *American Prospect*? The comedy is purely unintentional.

In campaigns, humor is the only thing that allows a candidate to escape the stifling pieties of politics. John McCain once alienated the single most powerful voting bloc in America and lived to tell about it, because although the joke he told was cruel ("The nice thing about Alzheimer's is, you get to hide your own Easter eggs"), it was also amusing.

For politicians, humor is freedom. Al Gore finally seemed to learn this two years after he lost the presidential election. But it was too late. Hours after delivering a winning performance on *Saturday Night Live,* he left politics for good.

Congressman Jim Traficant has also left politics for good, thanks to a series of bribery convictions and a long sentence in a federal prison. There's no politician I miss more. Traficant was a terrific guest not simply because he was compulsively outrageous and wore a hairpiece that looked like a raccoon, but because he was willing to appear on television drunk.

This is rarer than you might imagine. It's difficult for most people to think or speak clearly when they've been drinking. Only a relative few take the risk. I've seen Christopher Hitchens of *Vanity Fair* do it. I'm fairly certain a former chairman of the Republican National Committee showed up on our set once after multiple bourbons. Traficant was proud to be drunk on television. Shortly before he was indicted, the Ohio Democrat arrived for a live show blowing at least twice the legal limit. He was completely plastered.

Traficant maintained his usual form on the air. He yelled and interrupted and made vague but sinister-sounding threats. It wasn't until the commercial break that he lost control of himself. Tearing off his microphone, he bounded off the set and directly into our floor director, a girl of about twenty-two, one step above intern. "Give me a hug," he demanded, standing about an inch from her face.

What? she said, recoiling. "Give me a hug!" Traficant barked drunkenly. His toupee looked ready to pounce. The girl was terrified. "No," she said. Traficant exploded. "You goddamn communist," he yelled, then loped out of the studio.

After the show, we discovered that Traficant had headed to the makeup room, where he physically assaulted the makeup artist. She was still upset by the time I arrived. "He grabbed me," she said. She could hardly believe it.

Months later, facing sixty years in prison and $2 million in fines for racketeering, extortion, and bribery, Traficant came on again, this time safely by remote. It was obvious he missed the floor director and the makeup artist. "Tell the girls at CNN that if I get convicted, I'm going to be looking for conjugal visits." Days later, he was convicted. He hasn't called.

It was always acceptable to be amused by Jim Traficant, and I usually was. In television it's considered less acceptable to seem amused by the solemn news of the day. This has been a problem for me, as I've long been prone to what campus speech codes refer to ominously as "inappropriate laughter."

In the fall of 2002, what turned out to be a pair of snipers roamed the Washington area, murdering strangers for no apparent reason. We did countless shows on the subject: Who is the sniper? How can police stop him? Do gun control laws work? One night we interviewed a retired D.C. homicide detective named Ted Williams. The day before, a middle-aged woman had been shot dead at a Home Depot in suburban Virginia. Williams made the point that her death was particularly tragic, as the woman had recently overcome breast cancer. At least that's what he tried to say, I think. What emerged from his mouth was: "And the worst is, she'd just had breast implants."

There's nothing funny about murder, obviously. And there's nothing more unattractive than appearing to think there is. The pressure not to laugh was enormous. Which, of course, made it harder not to. I struggled to keep myself under control, fighting for calmness as my chest heaved with involuntary chuckles. I bit the inside of my lip, which worked momentarily. Finally, I lowered my head and tried to take deep breaths through my nose. The crisis passed.

Just about anything can trigger an on-air laughing fit: a strange turn of phrase, an absurd argument, a guest who clears his throat in a particularly gurgly way. I have a particular weakness for people who refer to themselves in the third person. For some reason this always evokes a vivid mental picture of Fidel Castro haranguing the masses for hours at a time in some square in Havana. It's a hilarious image (if you're not among the masses being harangued) and it invariably makes me laugh out loud.

So does the phrase "electrical college." I never knew this until the Florida recount, when at least one guest in five would take a verbal tumble on the way to pronouncing Electoral College. I always wanted to respond with a line about plumbing or carpentry. I never did, though. That would be mean.

As painful as they were, there was something undeniably funny about the final days of the 2000 election. The chaos created a void into which the usual freaks, extremists, and discontents of the political fringes assembled. Deranged political people crack me up. My favorite moment was the night of the final Supreme Court decision, and not just because Bush won.

Bill Press and I did *Spin Room* from the park across the street from the court that night, mostly because the Supreme Court building looked terrific in the background. Unfortunately, because the court's decision had arrived unexpectedly, we hadn't had time to book guests. With an hour of air to fill, our producers desperately combed the crowd for people to interview. They found a couple of them. The first was Governor Bill Owens of Colorado, who had nothing really to do with the story but was well-known enough (in our judgment at the time anyway) to talk credibly about politics. Still, it dawned on me that viewers might be confused as to why we were talking to him. So as I introduced Owens, I mentioned that we had found him hanging around the park and asked him to drop by the show.

Next up was a member of Congress, a nice guy who, as most people in Washington know, is gay. Apparently, most people in his district do not know this. Seconds before we came back from a commercial, the congressman turned to me with an anxious look on his face. "Do me a favor," he said. "Please don't say you found me hanging around the park."

I had barely finished fighting back the involuntary laughter when a protester showed up. A middle-aged man with wild hair, he stood silently behind us holding a sign with a Web site address and an unintelligible message about government reform. (I never discovered whether he was for it or against it.)

For some reason, it suddenly seemed like a good idea to ask the guy a few questions, pull him into the show, get interactive with him. It only took one question for him to go completely berserk. He started shouting and waving his sign. We tried to end the conversation.

But he kept shouting. He was still shouting when we came to a commercial. I turned around and asked him to shut up. He wouldn't. I suggested he perform an anatomically impossible sex act. He started screaming something about the First Amendment. This set me off. If you yell during the next segment, I said, I'll kill you. Suddenly, he looked surprised. "Are you threatening me?" Not really, I thought, but that sounded lame so I didn't say it. I turned back around and tried to ignore him.

The protestor didn't say much more after that. I figured he'd gone home. He hadn't. He'd gone to find the police. I was taking off my microphone when two cops came up. "He says you threatened him," said one, pointing to the protestor. I gave the cop a you've-got-to-be-kidding-do-I-look-violent? look. He nodded. He understood. He'd seen it before. *Another sign-carrying wacko making wild allegations.*

This, I was pleased to see, drove the crazy guy even crazier.

He yelled at me as I walked to my car. "See you in court! I'm going to slap a defamation suit on you!" He wagged his sign like a scolding finger. "I hope you're a lawyer!"

I didn't take it personally, and I hope he didn't, either. I like enthusiastic political activists. One of the best things about politics is the costumes. During the New Hampshire primary, people with obscure positions and grievances (For the Gold Standard! Against Circumcision!) routinely wander into town halls and candidates' forums dressed in bizarre outfits. At a single event, a man opposed to commercial fishing will arrive dressed as a shark, while across the room a guy with a boot on his head and a pair of swim fins glued to his shoulders like epaulets will be handing out literature for the Free Dope party. It's like the circus, except it's free.

These aren't necessarily people you'd choose to have dinner with. But from a safe distance, it's easy to admire their dedication, and the unsullied purity of their beliefs, ludicrous as they may be. As long as they're not in power, activists are good for a political system. True believers remind both parties what they stand for. Unfortunately, they're disappearing, particularly on the Left.

Phil Donahue is one of the few who remain. After the 2000 election, the longtime talk show host came on *Crossfire* to defend his support of Ralph Nader. Many Democrats were furious at Donahue for helping to defeat Gore. Donahue didn't care. He didn't seem particularly upset that George W. Bush became president. Donahue recognizes few distinctions between the two major parties, but if forced to choose he probably dislikes the Democrats more.

"McAuliffe and company," he calls them. "The corporate-money-besotted Democratic party." His eyes bulge when he talks like this. He doesn't blink. If there's one thing that makes

Donahue mad, it's the fact that Big Business runs the country. In the tiny world where Phil Donahue resides—at the leftward terminus of American politics—"we don't think corporate power is good, as both parties feel. . . . No, no, no." Nor does Donahue believe that capitalism is a fundamentally benevolent system, or that encouraging a free market is the most democratic means of arranging a society. Donahue considers these notions propaganda, spread by the "industrialists."

My first thought was: What an odd thing to say. When was the last time you heard the word "industrialists" used as an epithet? It has the flavor of a Rockwell Kent painting or a tract by William Z. Foster, as outdated as it is unfashionable. My second thought was, where were people like Phil Donahue during the Clinton years? Throughout the 1980s, it was easy to find liberals willing to criticize the market, or even to question the basic assumptions of capitalism. Then, on about January 20, 1993, they seemed to vanish.

Almost immediately after Clinton's inauguration, you stopped hearing mainstream liberals talk about the poor and the homeless and the tragedy of income disparities. For the most part, liberals sat by quietly as the country got welfare reform and NAFTA. In general, there was a dramatic reduction in whining about the unfairness of American society. Most of these changes were good.

But not all. Class-warfare liberalism may have been infuriating and divisive, but it served a purpose. Greed isn't a positive thing. Liberals used to say this. Accumulating wealth for its own sake is a pretty boring way to spend one's life. Liberals pointed this out, too. Selfishness is bad. Making money doesn't make you heroic. These were valuable sentiments.

So, it turns out, was liberal guilt. During the Clinton years, liberals seemed to stop feeling guilty about anything. New-economy liberals were the least guilty of all. The very month the NASDAQ crested, I had dinner with a group of rich dot-com types in San Francisco. All were liberal Democrats. One of them, Chris Larsen, the CEO of the on-line lending company E-Loan, explained that he didn't feel guilty at all about any-thing. Guilty rich people, he said, are "fucked up."

Larsen could say this because, despite his own tens of mil-lions, he didn't consider himself a Rich Guy. Fit, wiry, dressed in a T-shirt and jeans, he was in his late thirties but could pass for a college student on the six-year plan. Like many high-tech executives, Larsen was quick to draw distinctions between his own future-defining company and the brick-and-mortar firms still tethered to the industrial age.

In the tech world, for instance, hardly anyone wore a tie. The few who did were mostly financial types and were derided by the rest as "suits." (In dot-com America at the peak of the boom, informality was the standard, and the standard was rigid.) As a sign of their egalitarian, nonhierarchical business philoso-phy, tech executives used only their first names in their E-mail addresses (bob@ehype.com). Everyone spent a lot of time talk-ing about "tearing down institutions," and "empowering the consumer." All of this allowed people like Larsen to think of themselves not as robber-barons-in-training, but as digital revo-lutionaries. At one point it even allowed Larsen to boast of his company's efforts to subvert Big Business.

Big Business? Aren't *you* Big Business? I asked. Larsen snorted. Look at me, he said without saying it. I'm no plutocrat. I wear rock-climbing shoes.

Is Chris Larsen an improvement over the stereotypically guilt-ridden liberals of the 1970s? Maybe not. Annoying and silly as it can be, guilt does provide some perspective. Without it, it's easy to believe that you deserve what you have. If you believe you deserve what you have, you could come to think that the more you have, the more deserving you are. From there it's all downhill to the obvious conclusion: The people with the most are the best people.

Until Enron, even many journalists bought this idea. A lot of reporters seemed to suspend disbelief entirely, sucking up to corporate executives without apology. In the business press particularly, the 1990s amounted to a decade-long orgy of throne-sniffing and power worship.

Consider the treatment of a single fantastically rich guy— Nathan Myhrvold of Microsoft—in two stories that ran in *Fortune* at the height of the dot-com hysteria. In the first, from July 1998, we learn this about Myhrvold: He is "a gourmand who loves French food." He "likes to laugh." He is brilliant, so brilliant that the federal government sees him as a threat. ("In essence," Myhrvold is quoted as saying without any clarifying commentary from the reporter, "the DOJ wants Microsoft to fire me so we can't innovate in products.") For vacation, Myhrvold plans to go "fly-fishing in Mongolia."

In the next *Fortune* profile, which ran the following July, we learn this about Myhrvold: He is leaving Microsoft. This is sad, since Myhrvold is a "smiling, cuddly" man with "many interests" who is "also clearly brilliant, charismatic, and up-front about being rich."

The last part is undeniable. Myhrvold spends a lot of the interview bragging about things he has bought recently. The interview itself takes place on the patio at Le Cirque. Myhrvold boasts that the kitchen in the vast new house he is building was designed by the same person who did the kitchen at Le Cirque. Except, Myhrvold says, "Mine's better."

The whole thing reads like a particularly fawning *Esquire* cover piece on Julia Roberts. But that's not the worst part. The worst part is, nobody seemed to notice. Nobody mocked *Fortune* for running it, probably because the same story could have run in virtually any other magazine in America.

It couldn't have run in *The Baffler,* though, except perhaps as a parody. During the 1990s, *The Baffler* may have been the most unfashionable magazine in America. As a publication dedicated to exposing "lies" like "the liberating promise of the cyber-revolution," it was totally out of step with its time. As a magazine that promised to "unmask the pretensions of the lifestyle liberals," it automatically alienated most of its potential audience. Needless to say, it's an excellent read.

The Baffler is edited by Tom Frank, an old-fashioned lefty intellectual who lives in Chicago. Frank's book, *One Market Under God,* makes many of the points that thoughtful liberals might have made during the 1990s, if they hadn't been corrupted by Bill Clinton and the easy money of the tech boom: Wealth is not an end in itself. The market is not the same as democracy. The diversity of choice and thought and experience that most people believe characterizes America is mostly an illusion. We think we're letting our freak flags fly. In fact, we all end up wearing J.Crew.

It's easy to argue with many of Frank's points. Like most people, he's better at diagnosing problems than proposing solutions. (Which in this case would be . . . what? Stronger labor unions? Socialism?) But Frank's instincts are hard to dislike. He is against conformity and sameness. He is for the individual. He thinks Disney is creepy.

I once called Frank at his office to find out if there are any liberals left in America who agree with him. Hold on a sec, Frank said. He shouted across the office: "Who in the worlds of politics or academia shares our views?" There was silence for a moment, then a muffled reply. Frank came back on. "I don't know," he said. "I'd have to think about that." A few minutes later, he threw out the titles of a couple books I'd never heard of. He mentioned a relatively obscure academic and some "pranksters" on the Web. Our position "doesn't make its way into mainstream media very much," Frank conceded. "We're basically all alone in this project."

There has always been a pronounced strain of flakiness in liberalism. In the mid-1930s, George Orwell famously described his fellow socialists as "that dreary tribe of high-minded women and sandal-wearing and bearded fruit-juice drinkers who come flocking towards the smell of 'progress' like bluebottles to a dead cat." But in recent years, that element—what Orwell called the "more-water-in-your-beer reformers"—has completely taken over. If you want to know how frivolous contemporary liberalism has become, look no further than its signature issue, the war against smoking.

In the spring, schools across America observe Kick Butts Day, an annual celebration of "tobacco control youth activism." The event was founded by Mark Green, the perennial candidate for mayor of New York City. In the early 1980s, Green was among the most promising liberals in the country. Smart, articulate, endlessly energetic, he might have done something important with his life. Instead, Green devoted his time to a series of microscopic initiatives designed to force other people to sit up straight and eat their peas. Whether they want to or not. Mark Green has become a public nanny, a carping neopuritan of the most severe and unforgiving kind. Kick Butts Day is his crowning achievement.

With their hair-trigger instinct for moral outrage, children make particularly fervid reformers, so it's not surprising that there is an authoritarian quality to many Kick Butts Day festivities. Students are encouraged to rat out their peers for smoking. Schools conduct "undercover" buying operations, designed to punish convenience store clerks (usually hapless immigrant minimum-wage workers) for selling cigarettes to minors. And so on. At one Ohio high school in the late 1990s, students gathered in the cafeteria to physically assault a mannequin dressed as a cigarette.

It is parents who smoke, however, who receive the roughest treatment from antitobacco zealots. Telling young children that their parents will soon die horrible deaths from smoking has long been a favored approach of school nurses. The discovery of secondhand smoke, though, has changed the calculation. Parents who smoke, it is now explained to children, are not only poisoning themselves, they are also poisoning their kids. A public service announcement released by the California Department of Health Services makes the point explicitly. Titled "Daddy's Girl," the radio spot opens with a daughter's voice addressing her father: "Daddy, this is your little girl. That's right, the same little girl you used to bounce on your knee while you watched football. Well, I've been meaning to ask you something all of these years: Why are you trying to kill me? That's what you're doing, you know, when you smoke those dumb cigarettes."

And just in case that's too subtle, children can hear the same message in rhymed verse from Sterlen Barr, perhaps the nation's preeminent antitobacco rap artist. Barr is part of the new industry of consultants, educators, and freelance activists-for-hire that has grown around the nonsmoking movement. (Tobacco companies aren't the only ones making a profit from cigarettes.) Barr says the student audiences he speaks to up to three times a week almost always appreciate his antitobacco rap. It begins: "The tobacco industry, they're not people who care. They get about one million teens to start smoking every year. Only thing they care about is how to make some more cash. Once you get addicted to the drug they all get a laugh."

I interviewed Barr once, mostly because I couldn't resist. (Antitobacco rap music? The very existence of the genre compelled an investigation.) Barr sounded grateful to have found his niche. Top antitobacco rap artists, he said proudly, "can get anywhere from $1,500 to $2,000 a day, on up" working the school circuit. "If you get in the right situation, you can do very, very well with it." In college, Barr studied chemistry with plans of going to pharmacy school. Then came the war against smoking. "I've created something where I can make a lot more than a pharmacist. Isn't that awesome?"

Barr was able to skip pharmacy school because, at some point, cigarette smoking crossed the threshold from a health issue to a moral one. As a television commercial created for the state of California's antitobacco program puts it, smoking harms a person's lungs, "but where it hurts most is in the soul." Smoking is now considered so sinful that even dying from it doesn't erase the shame. In a 1994 paid obituary from the *Arkansas Democrat-Gazette*, for instance, the grieving relatives of a forty-six-year-old man made certain to explain that he had died after "a long heroic non-smokers battle with lung cancer."

Since smoking is now viewed as a soul-imperiling flaw rather than just a dangerous habit, it's not surprising that many of those who oppose it speak with absolute moral certainty about their cause. Bill Novelli, the founder of the Campaign for Tobacco-Free Kids, sounds like a Baptist preacher on the last night of revival week when he talks about cigarettes. He makes no apologies about using children as weapons in what he calls the Tobacco Wars. "These kids are advocates," he says, explaining why so many second-graders have become energetic lobbyists for tougher tobacco legislation. "I don't think it's a question of manipulating children or using children at all. I think it's a question of children taking their natural bent. Many of these children want to do that."

An eight-year-old's "natural bent" is political activism? This may be true (judging from the behavior of the Red Guards and preteen members of the Khmer Rouge, it probably is). But that doesn't mean adults with a political agenda ought to take advantage of it, exploiting the self-righteousness of children to achieve some legislative goal or other.

People shouldn't smoke. Almost everyone agrees. But liberals have taken this piece of commonsense medical advice and elevated it to a crusade, an excuse for moral exhibitionism, almost a worldview. There's nothing wrong with being opposed to smoking. But if that's the strongest moral message you've got, it may be time to rethink your politics.

On the other hand, antismoking activists make great television. So do the animal-rights types, people for whom eating a hamburger is ethically equivalent to firebombing a day-care center. This is another group whose world contains not a single shade of gray: The lives of all breathing things have precisely the same value. A rat is a chimp is a baby.

That's what they say. Privately, though, I sense they prefer the rats and the chimps. I've never met an animal-rights activist who wasn't strongly in favor of abortion—for people anyway.

In any case, they're interesting to watch, in the way that all unyielding people are. Ingrid Newkirk, president of People for the Ethical Treatment of Animals, may be the most entertaining. If there was ever a person who illustrates the distinction between animal-rights people and people who love animals (the first group likes the idea of animals; the second has them sleep on the bed), it's Newkirk. Newkirk has dedicated her life to protecting species of all kinds. Yet, she told me once, she does not personally have a pet. No dog. No cat. Not even a goldfish. She doesn't "have time," she said.

It was like finding out that the chairman of Ford drives a Subaru. Or that the president of Mothers Against Drunk Driving carries a flask in her car. It's a fistfight at a pacifists' convention. It's deep comic irony. Somehow it confirmed everything I'd suspected.

For sheer moral certainty, though, it's hard to beat the professional campaign finance reformers. There's something about campaign finance reform that can give otherwise normal people a faraway look. Warren Beatty once kept me on the phone for more than an hour speechifying earnestly about why all federal campaigns should be paid for by tax dollars. It was a beautiful day in Los Angeles, and I wondered: Doesn't he have anything better to do? You'd think a guy with his hobbies could find something more interesting to talk about. Then it struck me: To Beatty, nothing was more interesting, because nothing else unraveled so many vexing and seemingly unrelated mysteries. Nothing else shed so much light on the way the world works.

This is the beauty of campaign finance reform as a theory: It doesn't just explain why lobbyists exist. It explains why bad things happen. It is a theological concept. It is the Theory of Everything.

Look at it right, and there is almost nothing imperfect or unjust about American society that can't be understood as the result of campaign donations: Pollution. Low test scores. HMOs. Racial tension. Lopsided tax cuts. Global warming. Decaying inner cities. In every case, these are evils visited upon America by bad campaign finance laws. It's that simple. Ask the campaign reformers. They'll tell you so, without embarrassment.

At some point, you begin to wonder if this is really a debate about public policy, or if it's a denomination. Administer the test yourself: Next time you read a piece about the effect of money in politics, replace the phrase "permissive campaign finance laws" with "malevolent spirits." You'll find that the tone and logic of the story remains essentially unchanged.

It's not all superstition, of course. Individuals and corporations and ideological groups do use money to influence legislation. This is a frustrating thought. But does it mean that democracy is a sham? And even if it does, what do you do about it? Ban certain forms of political advertising? Publicly finance all campaigns, as many good government groups advocate?

Maybe. But first you have to answer a series of other questions: What about the First Amendment? How is it that Americans, even those who work for labor unions and big businesses, suddenly don't have a constitutional right to express their political views through advertising? And if you use tax dollars to fund campaigns, who decides which campaigns are worth funding? And what about candidates who want to fund their own campaigns? How could you prevent them from doing it?

It's not a conspiracy of moneyed special interests that has prevented meaningful campaign finance reform. It's the details. They're complicated. Not that you'd know that from talking to the reformers.

I've talked to a lot of them. I even had the privilege of spending most of a weekend with ninety-one-year-old Doris Haddock, the campaign finance reform movement's most revered living icon. In the mid-1990s, Haddock was widowed and living in New Hampshire, a retired shoe factory employee surviving on Social Security. One morning she read an op-ed in the *Boston Globe* about the political influence of the tobacco industry. Intrigued, she began collecting more stories about campaign finance reform. She filled one scrapbook, then another. She got in touch with Common Cause.

Before you could say "mission from God," Doris Haddock had a new purpose in life: to wake Americans to the corrupting influence of big money in politics. She changed her name, adopting the *nom de reform* Granny D. She then decided to stage a kind of protest march across the United States. Starting in Palo Alto, she walked east, ten miles a day, six days a week, until she reached Washington, D.C. The trip took fourteen months. She stopped in virtually every town along the way to recite the Nicene Creed of campaign finance reform. At the end of the journey she produced a book, later published by Random House for a six-figure advance.

It was an impressive feat by any measure, and a remarkable one considering her age. Granny D. was really, really old. She graduated from high school during the Coolidge administration. She didn't ride in an automobile until she was thirteen. Her daughter has Alzheimer's. Granny D. herself had emphysema (she smoked Salems for fifty years) as well as arthritis, and the general frailty that comes from living for most of a century. Under other circumstances, she would have been in a nursing home. Thanks to campaign finance reform, she got around like a fit seventy-year-old. The desire to separate money from politics filled her like a life force.

By the time I met her, Granny D. was on the road again. She had returned to Washington to lead rallies in support of the McCain–Feingold campaign finance reform bill. I figured she'd be a good interview. The guy who was handling her press agreed. "Why don't you bring her back to your house?" he said. "That way you couldn't skewer her too much once your family fell in love with her."

I thought he was kidding. He wasn't. The next night, Granny D. was standing in my living room. She looked every bit like someone who has just crossed the continent on foot. Wearing a straw hat and wrapped in a shawl, she was festooned from head to toe in beads, rawhide, eagle feathers, and political buttons. My kids were fascinated. Three of them gathered around her in their pajamas, staring. I could tell they wanted to ask her about the feathers. Granny D. wanted to talk about the McCain–Feingold legislation. She was still talking about it when the children finally padded upstairs to bed. My kids, I discovered, aren't interested in campaign finance reform.

The next day, Granny D. and I headed to the Capitol, where she was scheduled to appear at a rally. There were no children at the event, only people consumed with campaign finance reform.

In this environment, Granny D. was a bona fide hero, the Che Guevara of the good-government Left. (Che himself is still the Che of the hard Left.) Speaker after speaker slobbered all over her. One described her as the "voice of the people," as well as the "personification of democracy," a moral figure on par with Dorothy Day, Eleanor Roosevelt, and Rosa Parks. Someone else compared Granny D.'s "presence" to that of Martin Luther King Jr.—one degree from holiness.

To her credit, Granny D. looked embarrassed, like she thought she was being taken too seriously. I was reminded of something she had said the night before. At dinner she had been telling me about what a wonderful experience it had been to walk across the country. "It was fun," she said, "certainly more fun than staying home in Dublin, New Hampshire, playing Scrabble with the shut-ins."

I think Granny D. really did care about campaign finance reform. I also think she was looking for a reason to get out of the house and meet new people. I couldn't hold it against her.

After food, water, and sex, the strongest human desire may be for someone interesting to talk to. It's what drove me to journalism, and what keeps me there. When you work on a talk show, the parade of characters never ceases. Sometimes they make up stories, or brag about themselves, or try to shout you down. I enjoy interviewing them anyway. It's definitely more fun than playing Scrabble with the shut-ins.

Where Does the
Opposition Party Sit?

✳   ✳   ✳

Alan Keyes is such a great speaker that he makes his own staff
cry. In 2000, Keyes, a longtime conservative activist and professional candidate, ran for president for at least the second time.
Just before the Iowa Caucuses that year, I went to see him deliver
his stump speech in a college gymnasium in Council Bluffs. Keyes
was late, so his political director warmed up the crowd. Midway
through his description of what Keyes was going to say, the man
burst into tears. Just thinking about Keyes's eloquence made him
weep. Keyes finally arrived and went on to give the single best
speech of the entire 2000 presidential campaign.

Actually, that isn't quite right, both because *every* Alan Keyes
speech is the best speech of whatever campaign he happens to
be running in and because what Keyes does is so different from a

conventional political performance that it's not fair to compare him to anyone else.

A Keyes speech doesn't open with jokes. It isn't held together with anecdotes about Ordinary Americans and the problems they face. It contains almost no biographical information about the man giving it. And, of course, it is never written down. Keyes speaks without notes—always—and in two or three hours onstage orating and answering questions he is unlikely to utter a single phrase that isn't grammatically perfect. He routinely launches into sentences so complex, with so many independent clauses, that no ordinary person could complete them without a written diagram. Keyes does it every time. He never says "um."

Most unusual of all, a Keyes speech rarely mentions politics, at least as most people understand it. Like all great speakers, Keyes is a preacher. His rallies are religious revivals, down to the passing of the plate at the end of the service. (In Keyes's case, the hat is usually a plastic jug stuffed with bills.) Keyes doesn't bother to give sermons on policy minutiae. Instead he begins with a topic like "The Purpose of Government," moving fluidly to "The Meaning of Liberty" before winding up in an extended rumination on "The Relationship Between God and Law." Almost everything Keyes says is totally abstract—a violation of Rule One of political oratory—but perfectly comprehensible. And not at all boring. Audiences are spellbound.

At least they were on the campaign trail. Keyes got a different reception not long after the election when he became a talk show host. Someone at MSNBC decided that Keyes's oratorical skills might be transferable to television, and so a show was created titled (ironically or not, it was never clear) *Alan Keyes Is Making Sense*. The program turned out to be as weird as its host. For an hour a night, Keyes lectured guests and viewers on his views about God, politics, and the world. He wore a sweater on the air. He paused for long periods of time, staring at the camera. Tics that came off as charming or impressive in speeches seemed almost terrifying in the context of a talk show. The ratings were terrible. Soon Keyes was back in private life, preparing for another campaign.

And that's too bad. Keyes is so talented, it's a shame he runs at all. There's something humiliating about hopeless candidacies. No matter how obvious it is that you're going to lose, you still have to pretend in public that you're going to win. It's enough to erode anyone's self-respect after a while. Why does Keyes do it? Running for president boosts his speaking fees in the off-season, of course. But I don't think that's the main reason. I think Keyes runs because, despite the occasional humiliations, campaigning is still more fun than anything else he's likely to be doing.

Plus, Keyes likes to show off. His better-funded opponents know this, and in 1996 they succeeded in excluding him from the first Republican primary debate. Keyes immediately played the race card, accusing the debate's sponsors of trying "to stand in the schoolhouse door and tell me I can't participate in this process." When that failed, he went on a hunger strike. Three days later, an Atlanta TV station (which Keyes described as a "tyrannical television station") barred him entry to the next debate. After two attempts to storm the studio, Keyes was led away in handcuffs. "My crime is being qualified to be president," he yelped.

At some point, the people who plan the debates decided that keeping Keyes out wasn't worth the effort. In 2000, he appeared at all seven. People used to say that George W. Bush looked inarticulate sharing a stage with Al Gore. I always thought Keyes made Bush look worse.

Consider their relative responses to a single question during the primary debate in Michigan. Moderator Tim Russert asked each of the candidates how the United States should respond to AIDS in Africa. "I think this is a compassionate nation," Bush replied, "and I think we ought to rally other compassionate nations around the world to provide the money to help the folks in Africa." Bush went on to point out that "this is a compassion-ate land and we need to rally the people of compassion in the world to help when there's a terrible tragedy like this in Africa."

When the question came to him, Keyes, who speaks six languages and wrote his Harvard Ph.D. thesis on Alexander Hamilton, seized the opportunity to expound on the role of licentiousness in the global moral crisis. It's a crisis that money cannot solve, Keyes said. "I think that this whole discussion is based on a premise that reveals the corruption of our thought." The audience applauded.

Keyes's poll numbers never rose above negligible. Any other candidate in his position would have been grateful for the free airtime. If Keyes was, he didn't reveal it. In debate after debate, he came off as dismissive and aloof. Often he implied that the moderators must be stupid. In South Carolina, Keyes was asked to name his biggest mistake. "I think about the biggest mistake I might make as an adult would be to treat that as if it's a question that is appropriate to be asked," he said.

At the time, the conventional view among Republicans was that Alan Keyes had some sort of mental illness. (John McCain told me he didn't dare oppose Keyes's inclusion in the debates, for fear "he might chain himself to my front door.") But loony as he might have been, Keyes never seemed to delude himself into believing he was going to be inaugurated. The same cannot be said for Steve Forbes.

Like Keyes, Forbes ran for president twice, in 1996 and 2000. Like Keyes, he never had a shot either time. (Keyes and Forbes wound up in about the same place in the polls by the end of the 2000 primary season.) Unlike Keyes, Forbes spent more than $60 million of his own money losing. By the fall of 1999, Forbes had sold so many assets to finance his doomed presidential bids that he was no longer the majority shareholder of his own company.

He may have been too busy to notice. Forbes was the hardest-working footnote candidate in the race. An instinctively private person, he forced himself to give literally thousands of interviews during the 2000 campaign. He delivered countless speeches, did daily radio commentaries, and traveled to almost every state in the union, often by bus. (When he flew, it was commercial, since he'd sold his own plane.) Forbes virtually never took a day off.

The result looked very much like a real presidential campaign. Forbes 2000 headquarters took up an entire floor of a large office building in suburban Virginia. Inside, the operation was divided into official-sounding divisions: "Office of Coalitions," "Political Ops.," "Polling Division," "Budgeting," "Legal Office," "Finance," and so on. The people who worked there seemed to have no idea their candidate wasn't going to win. Every week, Forbes's staff would send out press releases with titles like "The Inaugural Debate of Campaign 2000 Showed Why Steve Forbes Is Going to Win." There was nothing ironic about any of it.

It didn't make sense. Steve Forbes the deluded single-digit presidential candidate bore no resemblance to Steve Forbes the laid-back magazine publisher I'd interviewed before the campaign. That Steve Forbes had no apparent pretense at all. He was charming in a dorky, self-deprecating way. He laughed and grinned and giggled a lot, often at himself. He talked enthusiastically about baseball. He had a funny haircut. He returned his own phone calls without the usual "please-hold-for-Mr.-Forbes" power displays. He did not, in short, seem like the kind of guy who would blow his inheritance ego-tripping through a midlife crisis.

Running for president did it to him. At some point during his first campaign, Forbes decided he could actually win. He came to believe in The Scenario, a Rube Goldberg–like series of events (a win in this state, a stumble by that candidate) that, if executed in sequence, will lead to victory. Predatory political consultants no doubt abetted this belief, but mostly Forbes convinced himself. Before long, he was addicted to campaigning.

This is not an uncommon addiction. In 1992, Pat Buchanan arrived at the same conclusion most talk show hosts come to sooner or later: I should be president of the United States. In contrast to most, he acted on it. Buchanan resigned from *Crossfire* and entered the race as a Republican, challenging then-president Bush for the nomination. He did surprisingly well. Four years later, Buchanan tasted victory, winning the GOP primary in New Hampshire.

And that's what sealed his fate. By 2000, Buchanan found he couldn't stop running. Campaigning for president had become a compulsion. The rationale for his candidacy, meanwhile, had all but disappeared. A number of committed social conservatives had already announced, Alan Keyes and Steve Forbes among them. Buchanan could no longer claim to be the one traditional Republican in the race. So he left the Republican party.

Where he wound up tells you everything you need to know about campaign addiction. Buchanan joined the Reform party, the last stop on the electoral crazy train. Founded by Ross Perot, the Reform party by 2000 had become little more than a collection of ideologically incompatible sects feuding over a pot of government campaign money. The most powerful of these sects was controlled by a militant leftist named Lenora Fulani. Buchanan quickly became Fulani's strongest ally.

Buchanan's plan was to use Fulani's support to win the Reform party nomination. Once he became the official candidate, Buchanan would receive millions in federal matching funds, which he could use to feed his campaign habit. It was a clever strategy, and largely successful. Unfortunately, it required Buchanan to ignore some of his most deeply held beliefs.

Like Buchanan, Lenora Fulani had also run for president before, only not as a Republican. Fulani had been the candidate of the New Alliance party, a group the FBI once described as "armed and dangerous" and a "cult organization." A longtime gay rights activist, Fulani had been active in Marxist and black-separatist causes for more than twenty years. She was close to Louis Farrakhan. She was adamantly pro-choice.

If Buchanan noticed any of this, he didn't say so. In fact, for the first time in memory, he didn't say much about social issues at all. Out of deference to his new friend, he adopted new campaign rhetoric, at least temporarily. Gone were his fiery paeans to the pro-life cause, as well as his trademark denunciations of homosexuality and libertinism. Buchanan even toned down his attacks on Marxism. The sad thing is, in the end he lost anyway.

But at least he beat John Hagelin, the other candidate for the Reform nomination that year. A stereo equipment manufacturer from Iowa, Hagelin was a veteran of at least two previous bids for the White House, both on the Natural Law ticket. As a disciple of the Indian guru Maharishi Mahesh Yogi, Hagelin espoused something called "yogic flying," an advanced form of transcendental meditation that its practitioners claim can free a person from the bonds of gravity. Hagelin spent much of the 1990s pushing the idea. "A permanent group of one thousand yogic flyers in Bosnia would solve the crisis there," he told one audience. "And a permanent group of seven thousand yogic flyers on each continent would put an end to all international conflicts and promote lasting world peace."

John Hagelin was a fringe candidate with a tiny potential base of support; you probably wouldn't consider voting for him unless you believed in yogic flying. But that wasn't the only reason the press ignored him. Political reporters considered Hagelin too far out to merit serious coverage. "Should we really pay attention to a guy this weird?" That was the feeling in the press corps. It always struck me as unfair. Hagelin was strange, though no more eccentric than Bill Bradley. The difference was, Bradley never got credit for it.

I never figured out why. It took only a few hours of traveling with his presidential campaign to conclude that Bradley was one strange guy. First and most obviously, there was the matter of his wife, Ernestine Schlant. Schlant attended many of his campaign events, always seated up front near her husband. Yet Bradley rarely introduced her or mentioned her in any way. Most women would be annoyed by this, and Schlant appeared to be no exception. She sat through his speeches with her arms folded tightly across her chest, looking angry.

I saw the couple interact in public only once, at a fund-raiser. Schlant introduced her husband, describing him as a strong but gentle person, someone who "sits there so demurely, so sweetly." Presumably this was meant as a compliment, but Bradley bristled as though he'd been insulted. "I have difficulty seeing myself as demure," he said tartly as he took the microphone.

Most candidates go to great lengths to hide their marital tensions. Bradley didn't believe in hiding anything. He often talked about the importance of being "true to who you are." He clearly meant it. Bradley was so true to who he was, he sometimes neglected to wear makeup before televised events. Onstage at the Beverly Hilton one night, Bradley's enormous, glistening forehead acted like a mirror, reflecting the spotlight like a beam across the ballroom. He looked like a human lighthouse.

It was a rare amusing moment in the campaign. For the most part, traveling with Bradley was like slow death. He made no effort to disguise his contempt for the press or for the political process itself. His speeches were so dull they constituted a form of aggression aimed at the audience: You are my captives. I can do to you what I will.

His press conferences were even weirder. Early in the 2000 campaign, I went to a "media availability" in downtown Los Angeles at which Bradley was scheduled to announce his position on gun control. Bradley arrived looking grumpy and distracted. With no introduction, he simply walked to the front of the room and launched into a sleepy monotone.

"I believe a national discussion and dialogue must begin on guns," Bradley said. "I think it's time to stand up to the National Rifle Association," while protecting "the rights of sportsmen and sportswomen." Blah, blah, blah, blah. He droned on. It was boilerplate, no different from what every Democratic candidate says in every forum when asked about gun control. The reporters were beginning to look almost as bored as the candidate himself. Then, without warning, Bradley pulled out a gun.

It was a Lorcin .380, a small semiautomatic pistol. Bradley waved it slowly around the room. Cheap, shoddily constructed "junk guns" like this, he said, are used in the "vast majority" of crimes. Eliminate junk guns and America will be a much safer country.

Bradley had no idea what he was talking about. Junk guns may be junky, but they're not the root of crime. According to the Bureau of Alcohol, Tobacco, and Firearms, the guns most frequently used to commit felonies are expensive and well made. But no reporter in the room asked Bradley to explain where he got his statistics. No one seemed to care enough. Even armed, Bradley had a narcotic effect on audiences.

Bradley himself seemed on the verge of unconsciousness. His eyelids drooped. His hand gestures suggested a man swimming through molasses. Any moment, I expected him to slip into a coma. Then a television reporter had the temerity to ask a question unrelated to gun control. Bradley came immediately to life. The question concerned a House vote that had taken place just the day before, but Bradley treated it as an outrageous non sequitur, as if he were being quizzed on the price of yak butter in Bhutan. "Well, I'm glad this is a conference on guns," he snorted. Until that moment, I never would have guessed that a man as tall as Bradley could come off as bitchy. It's possible.

Somehow moments like this never made it into most Bradley profiles. His dazzling résumé was part of the reason. Rhodes Scholar, Hall of Fame basketball player, three-term U.S. senator—Bradley on paper looked like an outstanding, utterly solid person. Very few observers seemed to understand how emotionally fragile he really was.

Al Gore understood, and he promptly went about exploiting Bradley's weakness. Gore knew that Bradley fancied himself a deep thinker on racial issues. It was never clear exactly what Bradley's thinking on the subject was—he was light on details—but he raised the subject constantly. He boasted about his black friends. He called for a "national dialogue" on race. He took every opportunity to exhibit his exquisite sensitivity to all matters of color.

Gore's response? He implied that Bradley was a racist. During the primaries, Gore charged that Bradley's health care plan would devastate minority communities. Why, Gore asked, would Bradley propose something so hurtful to African Americans? There was no explicit answer. But the implication was clear: Because Bill Bradley has a problem with black people.

Bradley went bananas at the charge. He huffed. He got red in the face. He could barely speak. When he finally did, it was to accuse Gore of lying about his health care plan, distorting his motives, and impugning his honor, all of which Gore had done.

Gore didn't even respond to Bradley's countercharges. Instead, he attacked Bradley for responding to his attacks with attacks. By the time it was over, Gore had launched two attacks to Bradley's one. Bradley, meanwhile, felt compelled to apologize for his lone, somewhat lame attack. And, of course, Gore was still attacking. Not to mention climbing rapidly in the polls. Bradley couldn't recover. Not long after, he left on an unusually long vacation and never returned to politics.

Bradley was easily rattled—one of the worst possible qualities in someone running for president. Protest candidates don't have this problem. If you're in the race to make a point about something larger than yourself, nothing can hurt your feelings.

Personal attacks don't sting. Instead, they're a symbol of your success, evidence that the Establishment feels threatened by your honesty. Defeat comes not as a blow but as a vindication of your belief that the system is rigged to exclude outsiders and mavericks. Losing is evidence you ran an honorable campaign— you were beaten because you wouldn't sell out to win.

Protest candidates really believe all of this—that losing is morally superior to winning—and that makes them wonderful subjects to cover, because it means they'll say almost anything they think. They tend to think some pretty unusual things.

During the 2000 presidential campaign, for instance, Ralph Nader ran under the banner of the Green Party USA, a straightforwardly socialist organization. The party platform called for a society that is "free of class distinctions," an America with "worker collectives" and guaranteed, high-paying jobs for everyone. According to the GPUSA, the federal government should confiscate and nationalize all banks, insurance companies, automakers, railroads, and energy utilities. It should also discourage the private ownership of land. Finally, the party demanded that the American military disarm and cease practicing violence.

Nader made a point of saying he didn't endorse every Green party position. He didn't have to. His own views were flaky enough. Nader's Web site, for example, devoted considerable space to exploring ways that marijuana can help save the planet. "Oil derived from the plant can be used for paints, sealants and plastics and a myriad of other products," the site explained. "Industrial hemp can be used to make high-quality paper and construction materials, sparing trees. Its fibers can be used in textiles as well. Along with a host of other plants, such as kenaf, industrial hemp has the potential to dramatically reduce our dependence on petroleum-based products."

Most people who talk about the wonders of environmentally friendly "hemp" are really just interested in being able to smoke pot legally. Not Nader. I'd be surprised if he's ever smoked it or done illegal drugs of any kind. In person, Nader is almost comically straight and serious. He wears a suit and tie at all times, including on the weekends. His sensibility is far more 1959 than 1969. You get the feeling the free love movement passed him by entirely.

A couple of years after he ran for president, Nader filled in as a guest host on *Crossfire* for a night. In the meeting before the show, Nader mentioned a commercial he'd seen the night before. It was an ad for Miller beer, in which two bikini-clad, silicone-enhanced models wind up rolling around in the mud and kissing. "I don't get it," Nader said with obvious bewilderment. "What do two women kissing have to do with beer? Do you think an ad like that really sells Miller?"

Nader may talk about revolution, but his personal attitudes are thoroughly bourgeois. Not so with his former running mate, Winona LaDuke, a Green party activist who lives on an Indian reservation in Minnesota. LaDuke promised that her first act as vice president would be to remove from the White House "the pictures of aging white men and put up pictures of women and people of color." (Down with George Washington, up with Grover Washington.) LaDuke didn't make it out on the campaign trail very much in 2000, probably because she was busy with problems of her own. Shortly before the election, her common-law husband, with whom she had a new baby, admitted that he owed more than $8,000 in child support payments to his other, legal wife and their three children.

LaDuke stayed home so much during the campaign that I don't think she ever received Secret Service protection. This put her in the minority of candidates. Typically, even the longest long shots get a detail of federal bodyguards after the New Hampshire primary. From that point until they lose, they are watched over like visiting dignitaries in a war zone. It's one of the greatest and most abused perks of running for president.

Toward the end of the 1996 race, Jack Kemp, then Bob Dole's running mate, made a brief stop in Chicago for a fundraiser. Local police closed the main highway in and out of the city during rush hour as Kemp's motorcade proceeded from the airport to a hotel downtown. Thousands of commuters missed appointments, showed up late to day care, or went without dinner so that Kemp and the reporters following him (of which I was one) wouldn't have to wait in traffic.

All of this was done in the name of security, though it was unlikely that anyone would have bothered to hurt Jack Kemp. Even if you disagreed with him, Kemp was hard to hate. And there was never much chance Kemp was going to find himself in a position to hurt anyone else. As he whizzed through Chicago a month before the election, even he knew he was going to lose.

No one complained about the roadblocks, though, at least not loudly enough to register. No one asked the obvious question: When did American politicians get the right to behave like members of a Third World junta, blockading intersections and blowing through red lights with armed entourages? No one asked, because no one seemed to care. It was as if voters had accepted the idea that the health and safety of a political leader should be the central concern of any city in which that leader finds himself. It struck me at the time as an odd attitude for a democracy.

But I recognized it. It's an attitude we're accustomed to in Washington, where the president rides to church in a sixteen-vehicle bulletproof motorcade. Presidents and other political leaders do get threats, of course, and after September 11 it's hard not to take them seriously. Still, most of the time avoiding danger isn't the point of a security detail. Displaying power is.

In Washington, the powerful have security protection. That's how you know they're powerful. In a city where even rich people don't drive particularly expensive cars, where a Lincoln sedan is considered a limousine, the real power move is not to own a Bentley. It's to be trailed by a Suburban with tinted windows. The mark of a successful Washington party is when the Secret Service sweeps your house beforehand.

It wasn't always this way. A month before the 1912 presidential election, someone tried to assassinate Teddy Roosevelt. The former president, then a candidate on the Progressive party ticket, was in Milwaukee for a speech. He had just finished dinner and was leaving his hotel when a bartender from New York named John Schrank stepped from the shadows and shot him. The .38 slug passed through Roosevelt's overcoat, a sheaf of papers, and an eyeglass case before smashing one of his ribs and lodging in his chest.

It was never clear why Schrank did it. Some newspaper accounts described a dream in which a ghost told Schrank to kill Roosevelt. Others said Schrank was angry that Roosevelt had decided to run again. (Schrank was, the *Washington Post* noted the following day, "apparently a fanatic on the third-term question.") Roosevelt himself did his best to pry a motive from the would-be assassin. After calming the crowd, which was eager to begin a lynching, Roosevelt summoned Schrank and demanded an explanation. Schrank wouldn't answer. Roosevelt got impatient and left to give his speech.

Roosevelt spoke for more than an hour, bleeding the entire time. Afterward, flagging from blood loss, he was taken to the hospital. But first he delivered some of the better lines of his career. "I will make this speech or die," he told his doctor on the way to the event. "I have just been shot," he informed the audience when he arrived, "but it takes more than that to kill a Bull Moose."

Theatrical? Sure. A pointless display of swaggering machismo? Absolutely. And for that reason, marvelous. Politicians don't act this way anymore, partly because physical courage is no longer a requirement for office, but also because it would be politically suicidal. A contemporary politician would destroy his political career by doing what Roosevelt did. His disregard for his own safety would be held against him, taken as evidence of recklessness, possibly of mental instability.

A modern candidate wouldn't even have the chance to address a crowd after being shot. His handlers, security staff, and personal trainers wouldn't allow it. A politician who tried to pull a TR would be tackled and, if necessary, beaten to death by his own bodyguards before reaching the podium. For his own safety.

Thanks in part to the wall of security that surrounds them, modern presidential candidates are almost completely cut off from the press. It's possible, even typical, for a reporter to cover a campaign for months and never learn what the candidate he's following is really like. This is frustrating for journalists and counterproductive for candidates. More access almost invariably produces more positive coverage. I've always thought that Pol Pot would have received better publicity if he'd given more interviews. Fidel Castro, meanwhile, proves you can put reporters in prison and still win the admiration of their colleagues, as long as you invite the press over for drinks once in a while.

Senator John McCain took this principle to its furthest

conclusion. McCain ran an entire presidential campaign aimed primarily at journalists. He understood that the first contest in a presidential race is always the media primary. He campaigned hard to win it. To a greater degree than any candidate in thirty years, McCain offered reporters the three things they want most: total access all the time, an endless stream of amusing quotes, and vast quantities of free booze.

The result was less like a conventional presidential campaign than a Grateful Dead show or a sophomore road trip to Vegas. It was addictive. I covered McCain on and off from the week he announced till the day he lost, and then some more after that. Like many journalists, I found myself completely sucked in, not simply by the candidate, but by the exhilarating experience of traveling with him. By the end I had trouble leaving the party.

On the afternoon of Super Bowl Sunday 2000, John McCain should have been nervous. The make-or-break New Hampshire primary was two days away. Most candidates would have been frantically trolling for last-minute votes or holed up in a hotel room somewhere refining strategy with their consultants. McCain was sitting on his campaign bus with thirty reporters, finishing off the second of two hamburgers.

McCain had just given a rousing speech to a packed New Hampshire VFW hall, and he was hungry. An aide had arrived with an appliance-sized cardboard box of McDonald's food. As McCain ate, dripping ketchup liberally on his tie, the aide tossed burgers over his head to the outstretched hands of the press. One of the burgers came close to beaning George "Bud" Day, a seventy-ish retired Air Force colonel who had been traveling with McCain. Around his neck Day wore the Congressional Medal of Honor, which he won for heroism during the years he spent with McCain in a North Vietnamese prison camp. "Where's the booze?" Day growled. Someone gestured to the back of the bus, and Day soon disappeared to rejoin a group of fellow former POWs who, by the sound of it, had already located the bar.

"Senator," said a reporter who had come on at the previous stop, "can I ask you a couple of questions?" McCain laughed. "We answer all questions on this bus. And sometimes we lie. Mike Murphy is one of the greatest liars anywhere." McCain pointed what was left of his hamburger at Murphy. "Aren't you, Mike?" Murphy, a thirty-seven-year-old political consultant who was both McCain's message guru and comic foil, nodded solemnly. "Murphy has spent his life trying to destroy people's political careers," McCain said. "I'll have yours done on Tuesday," Murphy replied.

The reporter looked a little confused but went ahead and asked his question, which was about McCain's strategy for winning the New Hampshire primary. Before McCain could answer, Murphy jumped in with his analysis. "The problem with the media," he said, "is, you're obsessed with process, with how many left-handed, independent soccer moms are going to vote."

McCain translated: "You're assholes, in other words." He chortled and grinned so wide you could see the gold in his molars. About this time, one of the POWs stuck his head into the compartment where McCain was sitting. Sounds of clinking glasses and raspy old-guy laughter followed him from the back of the bus. "We're picking your cabinet back there, John," he said.

The reporter never got an answer to his question, though it hardly mattered. After a day or two of this sort of thing, the average journalist inevitably concluded that John McCain was about the coolest guy who ever ran for president. A candidate who offers total access all the time, doesn't seem to use a script, *and* puts on an amusing show? If you're used to covering campaigns from behind a rope line—and all political reporters are—it was almost too good to believe. The Bush campaign complained that McCain's style and personality caused many reporters to lose their objectivity about him. The Bush campaign was onto something.

I saw reporters call McCain "John," sometimes even to his face and in public. I heard others, usually at night in the hotel bar, slip into the habit of referring to the McCain campaign as "we"—as in, "I hope we kill Bush." It was wrong, but it was hard to resist.

Thanks largely to the fawning press coverage he received, McCain won the New Hampshire primary in a nineteen-point upset. That night, the campaign threw a party, orchestrated by two heavily tattooed New York night club DJs, in the lobby of McCain's hotel. Hundreds of people came to shout and drink and celebrate. McCain himself slipped off into a conference room to do a series of postvictory television interviews.

Since no one stopped me, I followed him. Outside, people were dancing and yelling. Inside the conference room where McCain sat, all was dark and still. Cameramen and sound technicians fiddled with coils of wires on the floor. A photographer, exhausted from days on the road, had taken off his boots and was lying flat on his back asleep, surrounded by camera bags. A CNN crew worked to dial up the satellite link to *Larry King Live*.

McCain was oblivious to it all. He had his eyes locked, unblinking, on the blank camera in front of him. His teeth were set, his chin thrust forward in go-ahead-I-dare-you position. Between interviews, he maintained the pose. McCain looked on edge and unhappy, not at all like a man who had just achieved the greatest political triumph of his life. There was no relief on his face. Sitting in the dark waiting for Larry King, he seemed burdened, or at least bewildered. Something unexpected happened to John McCain: He won. He was the dog who caught the car.

It was close to midnight when we left the hotel for the Manchester, New Hampshire, airport and the flight to South Carolina. The staff bus pulled onto the tarmac and came to a stop beside an elderly looking jet with Pan-Am markings. Representative Lindsey Graham of South Carolina, who had spent all week stumping for McCain, spotted it through the window. He looked slightly concerned. I could tell what he was thinking: Didn't Pan-Am go out of business years ago?

"What kind of plane is that?" he asked Murphy. "It's a Russian copy of a 727," Murphy said. "It was decommissioned from Air Flug in the seventies. The Bulgarian mechanics checked it out and said it runs fine. We're not wasting precious campaign dollars on expensive American-made, quality aircraft. A minivan full of vodka and a sack of potatoes, and we got it for the whole week."

Murphy seemed to be joking, though over the next month, as the campaign traveled from coast to coast and back again and again, the plane did take on a certain Eastern European feel. The paint around the entryway was peeling. The bathrooms were scarred with cigarette burns. One of the engines periodically made loud, unexplained thumping noises. After a while I began to suspect that whoever was at the controls was dangerously new to the United States. As the plane touched down at a private airstrip in rural Ohio one afternoon, a voice came over the intercom with a disconcerting announcement: "Ladies and gentlemen, welcome to Indianapolis."

None of this bothered McCain, who had successfully bailed out of four airplanes and knew he wasn't going to die in one. (If the plane ever did go down, there would have been a stampede of people trying to hop into his lap.) McCain spent most of his time in the air asleep. Presidential candidates traditionally sit at the front of the plane, behind a curtain where they can confer privately with their staffs. McCain did very little in private. After each event he reboarded the plane like any other commuter, opened and closed a series of overhead bins in search of a place to store his coat, then found a seat in economy class and sprawled out, head back and mouth open. Before long he was snoring.

If it was after four in the afternoon, just about everyone else had a drink. Cocktails were a recurring theme on the McCain campaign. McCain himself rarely had more than a single chilled vodka. Members of his staff drank early and often, and were usually in the bar till closing. (When the bar at the Copley Plaza in Boston finally stopped serving one night, one of the campaign's traveling press secretaries went to his room, emptied the contents of the minibar into a pillowcase, and returned to keep the festivities going.) At the front of the plane, right outside the cockpit and across from the cigarette-burned lavatory, were coolers of beer and wine, surrounded by baskets of candy bars and plates of cheese cubes. At the back was a bar—not a rack of miniature airplane bottles, but a table laid out with quarts of booze, ice, and mixers. Minutes after takeoff, a crowd invariably gathered near the rear galley.

A cable news producer worked to wrench the cap off a beer bottle with a cigarette lighter as a group of cameramen sat nearby chatting and drinking champagne out of two-piece plastic cups. John Weaver, McCain's taciturn political director, spent most flights standing at the bar pouring himself drink after drink. In the row next to him was the campaign's advance team, usually busy stuffing confetti guns—thick plastic pipes with CO_2 canisters at the bottom—with orange streamers in preparation for the next rally. They were drinking, too. Off to the side, watching it all between long pulls on a Bud longneck, was Greg, the guy whose job it was to drive the bus when the plane landed.

Greg first signed on with the McCain campaign at the beginning of the New Hampshire campaign, when he was hired from a charter bus company in Ohio. He was thirty, a laid-back, chain-smoking Navy veteran with no interest in politics. Greg initially expected to be back home within a couple of weeks. That was in August. In December, he returned to Columbus briefly, got married, then left to rejoin McCain two days later. Over the next three months, he saw his pregnant wife for a total of twenty-four hours. After the New Hampshire primary, Greg was essentially kidnapped.

Like a lot of former fighter pilots, McCain was superstitious. He wore lucky shoes, ate lucky food, made certain to get up on the lucky side of the bed. His pockets were stuffed with lucky talismans, including a flattened penny, a compass, a feather, and a pouch of sacred stones given to him by an Indian tribe in Arizona. At some point, McCain began to suspect that Greg was a lucky bus driver. The campaign's poll numbers began to rise around the time Greg was hired, bolstering this theory. The nineteen-point blowout in New Hampshire proved it wasn't a theory at all.

In the weeks after, Greg went everywhere with McCain. Campaigns typically hire new bus drivers in each city. Those who travel stay in inexpensive hotels near the rest of the campaign staff. Greg stayed in McCain's hotel every night, sometimes in a suite. On the night of the Arizona and Michigan primaries, he was among the small group invited to McCain's house to watch the returns come in. When CNN announced that her husband had won both states, Cindy McCain turned immediately to Greg. "You're never going home again," she said, giving him a hug.

It occurred to me that if McCain ever did become president, he might appoint Greg head of Amtrak. If not secretary of transportation.

Not that Greg would have accepted. All the attention seemed to make him nervous. Or maybe Greg's drinking problem was preexisting. Either way, as the campaign dragged on, he retreated further and further into Budweiser. He was usually the first one to open a beer and the last one to stagger up to his room from the hotel bar. By the end, Greg often wasn't even behind the wheel of the bus. Not only was he too hungover to drive, he was too important.

Ultimately, I came to see Greg as a living metaphor for the McCain campaign: reckless, drunken, slightly demented. On the morning after he lost the South Carolina primary, McCain was scheduled to appear on *Meet the Press*. We were in Detroit by this time, and I rode with McCain as he drove to the television studio. He was in a great mood. As the bus rolled past miles of rubble-strewn vacant lots, McCain told story after story, winding up with a dramatic account of the time he watched an Indian woman give birth in the corner of a bar in New Mexico. He didn't seem upset about South Carolina. He hadn't come up with talking points to explain his loss there. He didn't appear to be preparing for *Meet the Press* in any way. McCain's aides weren't even sure how long he was supposed to be on the show. Half an hour? Fifteen minutes? No one knew. (The full hour,

McCain discovered when he got to the studio.) No one really cared, least of all McCain.

McCain wasn't much of a detail guy. He could do a pretty good campaign finance reform rap. He could talk forever about the need to open up Washington National Airport to long-haul flights to the West Coast. He seemed to know everything about American Indian tribes in Arizona. Venture far beyond those topics, and the fine print got blurry. As he explained to me once, there's no reason to get sucked into "Talmudian" debates over policy. "I won't bother you with the details," McCain often said when asked about a specific piece of legislation. "That's a very good question," he'd respond, and then neglect to answer it.

It was an effective technique before large audiences; most people don't really want to know the details. It didn't work as well on television. McCain had a pretty rough time on *Meet the Press* that morning. Tim Russert did want to know the details. McCain didn't have them. It was painful to watch.

McCain's aides, who were watching by remote from the next room, seemed totally unbothered. The political director didn't pay any attention at all. Instead, he was eating melon and chuckling about the campaign's new, unofficial slogan: "Burn It Down." "It's like Stokely Charmichael," he said. "Power to the people!" He threw his fist into the air. "Burn It Down—I love that."

I never learned exactly what "Burn It Down" was supposed to mean. I doubt McCain did, either, but he took the spirit of the slogan to heart nonetheless. At some point during his campaign, McCain decided that his real enemy was the Republican party. "My friends," he'd tell audiences, "my party has lost its way. My party has become captive to special interests." At first, the lines were uttered more in sorrow than in anger. After a while, it was mostly anger.

And it was real. More than a year later, I had dinner with McCain at a Vietnamese restaurant in suburban Virginia. By chance, it was the same night that Senator Jim Jeffords of Vermont had announced he was leaving the Republican party, thereby throwing control of the Senate back to the Democrats. It was big news, not least for McCain, who was going to lose a committee chairmanship because of it. McCain didn't seem to care. He was clearly pleased that the GOP was suffering. "Fuck them," was his attitude. He may even have said that out loud.

I don't know exactly when McCain came to loathe his own party. I first noticed it during the primary in South Carolina. Leaflets had been distributed at political events throughout the state savaging Cindy McCain for her early '90s addiction to prescription painkillers. No one took credit for them, though McCain blamed Republicans, and the Bush campaign in particular. "They're going around saying Cindy's a drug addict who's not fit to be in the White House," McCain said, his fists clenched. "What am I supposed to do? Come out and make a statement that my wife is not a drug addict?"

He was still brooding about the leaflets a couple of weeks later when the campaign plane touched down in St. Louis. McCain was in town for a few hours to participate by remote in his last scheduled debate with Bush. He and half a dozen advisers gathered in the conference room of a television station downtown to eat barbecue and prepare. "I've got to try not to get down into the weeds tonight," McCain said, to himself as much as anyone. Bush may be a dirty campaigner; on the other hand, "nobody gives a shit."

It was a good point, and absolutely true. Voters say they dislike attacks ads, but they generally believe them. They may feel sorry for a candidate who is being bashed over the head, but they tend to assume he must have done *something* wrong. And no matter how they feel about the accuracy of an attack, voters almost always perceive complaints about negative campaigning as whining. McCain knew all this. But he was still mad.

With three minutes to go before airtime, McCain stood in the makeup room practicing his final comments. Rick Davis, his campaign manager, paced back and forth nervously, humming "Ode to Joy." McCain used a thick blue marker to jot down some final revisions on a piece of scrap paper. Looking out across an imaginary audience, he tried to recite what he had written. "I am a proud Reagan conservative," he said. "I am . . ." He stumbled, stopped, then closed his eyes. For a moment he looked defeated, like he couldn't continue. "I'm drawing a blank," he said. Mike Murphy leaned forward until he was inches from McCain's face. "It's okay," he said softly.

And in seconds, it was. Soothing the candidate was a large part of Murphy's job. McCain loved funny stories, and during lulls in conversation on the bus he often asked Murphy to tell the one about working for Senator Larry Pressler, who was said to have Alzheimer's. Or about the campaign ad he once made that accused an opponent of selling liquor to children. As Murphy told the story, no matter how old it was, McCain always broke into hysterical, chair-pounding, hard-to-breathe laughter. McCain was genuinely amused by Murphy—he called him "Murphistopheles," "the Swami," or simply "008," James Bond's little-known political-consultant brother—but he was also calmed by his presence.

The debate went fairly smoothly for McCain, despite the obvious disadvantage of appearing by satellite. Afterward, as he sat in a chair having his makeup removed, Murphy rendered the verdict. "You were better than last time," he said. "You were good." "Do you think so?" asked McCain. It was not a rhetorical question. He wanted to know. "You were better and he was better," replied Murphy, "so it was sort of a blur."

It soon became clear that a blur was not good enough. McCain's poll numbers stalled. Republican primary voters were turned off by his attacks on their party. They didn't understand the "Burn It Down" talk. It made them nervous. Bush was cruising to an easy victory.

The end came five days later. At a quarter to eight on the night of the California primary, Tim Russert called McCain's suite at the Beverly Hilton to say that the latest round of exit polls from the West Coast looked bad. McCain had already lost New York and Ohio and a couple of other states. The networks hadn't called the race yet, but McCain wasn't one to drag things out.

"All right, Johnny," he said, looking around the room for John Weaver. As the political director, it was Weaver's job to arrange concession calls to the Bush campaign. Weaver hated doing it, and for the moment he had disappeared.

"Johnny," McCain called again.

Weaver's voice floated out of an adjoining bedroom. "Do I have to?" he asked. "Yep," said McCain.

A few minutes later, Weaver appeared with a cell phone. His mouth was puckered, like he'd just taken a shot of something sour. Bush was on the line. McCain took the phone without hesitating. He leaned back in his chair, feet on the coffee table in front of him, chilled vodka in hand, and congratulated the man he had come to despise. "My best to your family," McCain said. The conversation was over in less than thirty seconds.

And that was it—the end of John McCain's run for president. It was time to face the reporters waiting in the lobby, and from there on to the concession speech. For a moment the room was silent. A few of McCain's aides looked like they might cry. Not McCain. He was buzzing with energy. "Let's go," he said, bouncing out of his chair. "Onward."

I never made it to the concession speech. A friend from *TIME* magazine and I decided to have one last expense account meal before the campaign was technically over. We both felt sad about McCain's loss, not because either of us wanted him to be president (though I sometimes did) but because we understood we'd never cover another campaign as open as his. We were right. Soon after, I went on the road with Al Gore. I spent most of my time cordoned off in the press area. It was a waste of time. I was itching to do something interesting.

So was McCain. Within a few weeks, I got a call from one of his staffers. "We're going to Vietnam," he said. "Want to come?"

The ostensible purpose of the trip was to be in the country for the twenty-fifth anniversary of the fall of Saigon, on April 30. Actually, McCain was planning to leave Vietnam on April 28, in order to make it back to Washington in time for the White House Correspondents' Dinner. But never mind. Even a pointless trip to Vietnam was more fun than what I was doing. I called Tina Brown to see if she'd pay for it.

Tina was editing the now-defunct *Talk* magazine, a glossy general-interest monthly in New York. I was supposed to be one of the magazine's political correspondents. Tina had sent me out to cover McCain for months on end, at incredible expense, only to decide at the last minute that she didn't want to run a piece about him. It didn't bother me. I was more interested in the experience of reporting a story than in seeing the story in print. Tina was very enthusiastic about new story ideas. She thought a trip to Vietnam sounded great. I didn't even have to explain why I was going. Not that I knew.

McCain in Vietnam turned out to be a lot like McCain in Des Moines or Manchester or Dearborn. Still in campaign mode, he barreled around Hanoi in a minivan with a group of reporters, telling stories and giving speeches. Only his audience was different. One morning, McCain spoke to members of the National Assembly, the country's rubber-stamp version of a legislative body. In America, he told the group, politicians have to listen to their constituents. As an example, he recalled one voter who had suggested that Congress pass a law mandating oral hygiene. "As a father of four children," McCain joked, "I supported requiring Americans to brush their teeth every night."

He chuckled. The Vietnamese officials didn't. They looked contemplative. You could almost hear them thinking: Now *there's* an idea. I always wondered if after we left the country adopted a three-cavities-and-you're-out policy.

A few hours later, McCain met with the chairman of the National Assembly, the Vietnamese equivalent of the Speaker of the House. The chairman invited McCain and the reporters following him on a tour of the building's main chamber, a cavernous Soviet-style room with rows of wooden desks and a statue of Ho Chi Minh. He explained the protocol of the assembly hall: who sits where, who speaks, and in what order. The lecture went on for a while, until Howard Fineman of *Newsweek* broke in with a question. "Where does the opposition party sit?" he asked, deadpan. This time the Vietnamese did erupt into titters. Nervous ones.

It was one reminder that despite the good food and pretty scenery, Vietnam was still run by a Stalinist regime. The McCain statue was another. We visited it one afternoon, on the edge of a lake in downtown Hanoi. The statue sits on the site where McCain was dragged to shore after being shot down on a bombing run. He was stabbed and almost beaten to death by the mob that pulled him out of the water, though the inscription doesn't say that. It merely notes that on October 10, 1967 an "air pirate" named "Jchn Sney Macan" was brought down by the People's Defense Forces. The statue depicts McCain on his knees, surrendering. It is splattered with bloodred paint.

McCain didn't have much to say about the statue ("It was covered with bird shit last time I was here"), just as he generally doesn't talk much about his war record. But the story is never far from the surface. It's unlikely McCain ever would have made it near the Senate, much less mounted a respectable presidential campaign, without his years as a prisoner of war. It's also true that his story becomes more impressive the more you know about it.

A Navy flier and third-generation Annapolis graduate (fifth from the bottom of the class, his autobiography notes with pride), McCain was shot down on his twenty-third mission over North Vietnam. He had just finished bombing a power plant when what looked like a flying telephone pole smashed into his plane. It was a surface-to-air missile. McCain ejected at 450 miles an hour, crushing his knee and both arms.

Finally taken to a prison hospital, he languished in a body cast, sick and filthy, for months. Then, less than a year into his captivity, the North Vietnamese offered to let him go. Fellow prisoners urged him to accept—McCain was badly injured and had left a wife and three small children at home—but he refused, on the grounds that POWs should return home in the order they were captured.

He spent a total of five and a half years in camps, a good deal of it in solitary confinement. He was tortured repeatedly, often with ropes. His teeth were knocked out. He was hung by his broken arms. His bones were set at odd angles and without anesthesia. (To this day, McCain cannot lift his arms high enough to comb his own hair.) He had severe dysentery for more than a year. At least once, he attempted suicide.

McCain suffered a great deal in Vietnam, though not necessarily more than hundreds of other American POWs. The striking thing about McCain was that, despite the punishment, he never ceased being a belligerent wiseass. Dragged back to his cell after days of torture, he became famous among inmates for shouting colorful obscenities at his captors. He was arrogant and funny till the day he left.

On Christmas Eve 1968, McCain and his fellow POWs were herded into a brightly decorated room for a makeshift church service. The North Vietnamese had invited foreign journalists and camera crews to record the event. McCain was determined to spoil the photo op. According to Robert Timberg's account in *The Nightingale's Song,* McCain immediately began making a scene: " 'McCain, stop talking,' cooed a smiling guard called Soft Soap Fairy, aware that he was on camera. 'Fuck you,' said McCain, louder than before. 'This is fucking bullshit. This is terrible. This isn't Christmas. This is a propaganda show.' "

When a guard called "the Prick" scurried over to quiet him, McCain went absolutely bananas: "Fu-u-u-u-ck you, you son of a bitch," he screamed, hoisting a one-finger salute whenever the camera pointed in his direction.

McCain paid the price for his outburst. Yet, decades later, he rarely mentioned being tortured or lonely or depressed. Instead, he made being a POW sound like something you might want to do. "We had a good time in prison," he said. "People say prison was really hard. It was also a lot of fun. It was really entertaining."

McCain didn't say this in a tough-guy, love-the-smell-of-napalm-in-the-morning sort of way. He said it like he really meant it, like most of his memories from prison were happy ones. In his last years in North Vietnam, McCain was the designated movie-teller, charged with writing, directing, and acting out films for the men in his cell. "I told over a hundred movies," he remembered, "some of which I'd never seen." His favorite was *Stalag 17,* the 1953 thriller about Allied POWs who tunnel out of a German prison camp. McCain had just finished writing the script for that one—on toilet paper with a bamboo pen and cigarette-ash ink—when "the goddamn gooks came in and took three of the stars of the movie out of the cell." To be tortured, presumably. McCain didn't elaborate. He was laughing.

I saw one of the prisons where McCain was held, and it didn't look like a funny place at all. Hoa Lo, made famous during the war as the Hanoi Hilton, is a medieval-looking brick compound near the center of the city. Much of the original prison was torn down in the 1990s to make way for development. The portion that remains had been turned into a museum of French atrocities. There was a guillotine on display, leg stocks, and other instruments of colonial torture and repression, most of which were later used by the communists on their own enemies, though there was no mention of that.

Or almost no mention. In a tiny room toward the back,

there was a small exhibit dedicated to the American flyers once held at Hoa Lo. Inside a glass case, there was a volleyball net and other pieces of memorabilia designed to show that the happy POWs had enjoyed every possible recreational opportunity. "Though having committed untold crimes on our people," read a placard, "American pilots suffered no revenge once they were captured and detained."

Another display case highlighted religious freedom. "American pilots in Hoa Lo prison attending mass in the cathedral," read the caption beneath a very staged-looking photo of men standing in church. I looked closely and saw that one of the men had an odd look on his face. His right hand was raised, a slender middle finger draped defiantly across his chin. After a moment I recognized his expression. It was a suppressed grin. I've rarely felt as proud to be an American.

Three days later I was in Tan Son Nhut Airport in Saigon headed home. It was early evening, and I'd spent the afternoon drinking beer with friends on the roof of the Rex Hotel. Maybe for this reason I didn't immediately suspect a problem when the man at the immigration desk told me to wait and walked into another room with my passport.

He returned a few minutes later with a supervisor. "No stamp," said the man, pointing to my passport. His supervisor explained that my passport lacked the official entry seal all visitors get when they enter Vietnam. Somehow officials in Hanoi had forgotten to give me one. Or maybe I'd forgotten to ask. Either way, I didn't have the stamp. This meant that I couldn't get on the airplane.

It was the sort of bureaucratic catch-22 for which the Vietnamese are justly famous: Since I hadn't received the proper stamp when I'd entered, I wasn't technically in the country. And since I wasn't technically in the country, I could not legally leave. My only hope, the supervisor said, was to reenter Vietnam and receive the entry stamp I'd missed when I hadn't officially arrived the first time. He never explained how I was supposed to get back into a country I couldn't leave and wasn't in. He did say I'd have to go to Hanoi to do it.

At this point, McCain walked over. He bowed to both men and smiled. The supervisor smiled back. "He's only smiling because he's got you," McCain said to me out of the corner of his mouth. He turned out to be right. Nothing McCain said on my behalf seemed to sway either man. If anything, his arguments appeared to strengthen their resolve to keep harassing me.

It was a case of bad timing. Virtually everyone in Vietnam knows who John McCain is, and on this day many of them were mad at him. That morning McCain had given a press conference at which he'd said that, in his opinion, "the wrong side won" the Vietnam War. I wondered later what McCain was supposed to have said (the side that won knocked out his teeth), but it didn't matter. The remark offended Communist party members, apparently including the immigration police at Tan Son Nhut.

McCain left on his flight an hour later, along with the rest of the reporters on the trip. I was sad to see them go, but without a passport or plane ticket (both of which had been confiscated) I didn't have much hope of joining them. I spent the next several hours in a holding room being yelled at by a cop named Pham.

Pham was dressed in a khaki uniform with red stars on his epaulets. He had long lacquered thumbnails and a mole on his cheek with a two-inch black hair growing out of it. He was convinced I had sneaked into Vietnam for some illicit purpose.

He tried his best to make me sign a statement to that effect, a long handwritten document placed over a pile of duplicates and carbon paper. I didn't want to sign. He yelled. I yelled back. He screamed even louder. His eyes bulged. His hands shook. I could tell he was getting mad.

It probably would have gone on like this indefinitely, but a foreign service officer from the American consulate showed up and broke the stalemate. His name was Jim. Jim stood and watched my exchanges with Pham for a minute. Then he called me aside and whispered into my ear, "Do you know what drug-resistant tuberculosis is?" I nodded. "It's rampant in the jails here," he said. "And you're going to get it, if you don't start acting polite."

I started immediately (though I never signed Pham's paper). Soon Jim had negotiated my release from the airport, and we were in the car together, headed to a bar. On the way, he told me his life story. Before joining the State Department, Jim had been a parasitologist, which, he informed me, is someone who studies parasites. "I sat at a microscope all day in St. Louis staring at people's shit," he said. After seven years of that, he decided to become a diplomat. He prepared for the foreign service exam by reading back issues of *Foreign Affairs* at the library.

Jim was having a great time in Vietnam. His latest project was a study, funded by the U.S. government, on "sex workers" in the country. His field work consisted of going to hookers. He claimed his wife didn't mind. "Most Vietnamese women will have sex with you if you pay them," Jim said.

I woke up the next morning hungover, and still stuck in Vietnam. I wandered around Saigon for a while, thinking about what it must have been like for McCain to spend five and a half years getting yelled at by unreasonable bureaucrats with lacquered thumbnails. When I got back to the hotel, there was a message from the consulate. A friend at *Talk* had heard about my passport problem and had called Jamie Rubin, Madeleine Albright's chief deputy at the State Department. Rubin had issued a statement asking the Vietnamese government to let me leave. I was free to go.

My old friend Pham was waiting for me at the airport. He looked the same as he had the night before. In fact, he was wearing the same clothes, down to the same cheap ballpoint pen in his shirt pocket. His attitude was completely different. Someone in authority had corrected Pham's misperceptions, violently, by the look of it. Pham couldn't stop apologizing for his previous behavior. He called me "sir" twice a sentence. He insisted on waiting with me while I bought new plane tickets. He tried to carry my bags.

In the daylight, Pham seemed a lot more pathetic than menacing. His English wasn't very good, he explained, because in school Russian had been the only foreign language offered. No one cared about Russian anymore. His fluency in it was a useless skill, like barrel-making or operating a Linotype machine. He wanted to learn computers, he said. More than anything, he hoped to move to the United States some day with his wife and young daughter.

Pham waved to me as I walked up the steps onto the plane. He yelled something, too, though I couldn't quite make it out. I think he said, "Come back soon!"

The Dick Morris Suite

✳ ✳ ✳

It's no secret that scandals are good for the news business. I know firsthand. If O. J. Simpson hadn't murdered his wife, I probably wouldn't be working in television.

I'm not alone in that, of course. Probably 80 percent of the legal analysts you see on the tube today began their on-air careers talking about the bloody glove. But unlike them, I'm not a former prosecutor, or a law professor, or even an attorney. I don't know a great deal about the Simpson case and never did. I just happened to return early from lunch one day.

It was in the fall of 1995, and I was working as a writer at the *Weekly Standard* in Washington. I was heading back to my desk with a take-out hot dog one afternoon when I ran into the receptionist. She asked me what I knew about the O. J. trial. My instinct was to answer honestly ("just about nothing"), but for some reason I caught myself. I asked her why she wanted to know. Well, she explained, Dan Rather's booker just called looking for an O. J. expert to go on *48 Hours* tonight. Everyone else is still at lunch. Can you do it?

Within a few hours I was on my way to CBS in New York. I'd never been on television, so before I left, I asked a couple of TV veterans for their advice. They gave me some: Wear a dark blazer. Don't wear a white shirt. Sit on your coattails so your jacket looks crisp. Decide ahead of time what you want to say; then say it no matter what the question is. Pause two beats before you answer. And speak as slowly as you can. It makes you sound thoughtful.

I tried to remember these instructions on the train, but I was having trouble concentrating. The whole experience had raised troubling questions about the way the world works: What did I know about the Simpson case that the rest of the population didn't? Was I really the most qualified person to explain the effect of the trial on American society? If not, why was I pretending to be? And why was a major news network allowing me to do it?

I realized later that I had been applying print standards to television. (If I was writing a story on O. J., I thought, I definitely wouldn't interview me.) But print isn't television. Both are forms of journalism, just as jogging and roller skating are both forms of forward motion. They're not the same. They require different skills. They operate by different rules.

This all became clear to me when I got to the studio. CBS had assembled a roundtable to talk about the cultural significance of the Simpson case. In addition to me, there were a couple of newspaper columnists and Clifford Alexander, the former secretary of the Army. Alexander seemed like a nice guy. He immediately made me feel like an expert on the Simpson case. He knew less about it than I did. I wasn't sure if he even knew what O. J. had been charged with. He did fine on the show, mostly because he was able to explain clearly the few things he did know. I did fine, too.

I never did another show about O. J. Simpson. (After the *48 Hours* experience, I resolved not to talk about things I knew nothing about.) But I did do a lot more television. It wasn't that my one appearance had been a smashing success. The important thing was that it had happened. The world of talk show guests is like a closed union: You can't join unless you're already a member. Bookers resist booking people they've never seen on television. Conversely, once you've been booked you're bookable. The process is self-authenticating.

Scandals are one exception. When a scandal breaks, or something else dramatic, unexpected, and all-encompassing happens in the news, the normal rules are suspended. Bookers book who they can get. Hence my debut as an O. J. expert.

The first big sex scandal I watched unfold in Washington consumed Dick Morris. Morris, Bill Clinton's closest political confidant and consultant, was caught on film with a $200-an-hour prostitute at the Jefferson Hotel in Washington. The *Star* tabloid ran pictures of the two of them together, standing on the terrace of Morris's suite. The story appeared the week of the 1996 Democratic convention in Chicago. Morris immediately resigned.

Over the next weeks, details emerged. They were horrible. Morris had run up a $12,000 bill with the woman, a thirty-seven-year-old call girl named Sherry Rowlands. Rowlands, who later wrote a book about the experience, claimed that Morris was a committed foot fetishist who sucked her toes in between strategy calls to the president. Rowlands listened in as Morris talked to both Clintons about the Whitewater investigation. She then watched patiently as Morris crawled around the room on all fours like a dog and "danced like Popeye" in his underpants.

After the Starr Report, it all seems pretty tame. But at the time it qualified as a shocking scandal. (I remember being most shocked by the allegation that Morris had tried to stiff Rowlands on part of her bill.) No one ever asked me to appear on television as a Dick Morris expert, though several months later I did find myself at the scene of the crime.

On election day 1996, two political consultants I knew threw a party in room 205 at the Jefferson, the Dick Morris suite. Bob Dole was expected to lose that night, and the consultants, both Republicans, figured that the site of the crashing end of a successful political career would be the perfect place for an "It's Over" party. It was. People drank and posed for pictures on the famous terrace. Others reclined on what was said to be the actual Morris "foot couch." I had a great time.

Such a good time, in fact, that I nearly forgot I'd agreed to do a public radio interview on the results of the election. By the time I remembered, I was loaded. Oh, well, I thought to myself, I'm sure everyone else who covers politics has been drinking, too. I'm sure no one will notice. I found an unoccupied back bedroom and called the station. Some moron put me on the air.

"So, Mr. Carlson," began the host, "what's the mood in Washington?"

"Guess where I am?" I said. "I'm at the Jefferson Hotel. In the Dick Morris suite."

Silence.

"You know, Dick Morris? The president's adviser? Who got caught with the hooker? I'm in his room. I mean, he's not here. But this was the room where he was with the hooker. Before he got caught. I'm here."

It went on like this, though only for a short time. Within about a minute, the host was thanking me for my insights and trying to get me off the phone. It took me about four "Thank you, Mr. Carlson"s before I got the hint.

In light of all that has happened since, the Dick Morris scandal might be forgotten today if it weren't for Morris's later contributions to the art of scandal etiquette. More than anyone else, it was Morris who established the necessity of publicly conferring with spiritual advisers once you've gotten in trouble. The next time you see an embattled member of Congress ostentatiously drop by his pastor's house before he heads into the courtroom, you can thank Dick Morris.

Disgraced political leaders have long turned to loyal spiritual gurus—Richard Nixon had Rabbi Korff—but Morris created what has become the unchanging formula:

1) Choose your adviser. Religious leaders willing to be used as political props aren't hard to find. Still, it has to be the right sort of person, someone who is both nonjudgmental (or at least reluctant to judge your particular sin), and at the same time semiplausible as a moral figure. It doesn't hurt if the person is a member of a protected racial minority.

Morris chose Armstrong Williams. Williams, a black conservative radio show host, met all the criteria. Several years before, he himself had been in a scandal of sorts, when a male member of his staff sued him for sexual harassment, claiming that Williams pressured him to share a bed when they went on trips together. Williams never admitted wrongdoing. But the cloud that hung over him made it unlikely that he'd condemn Morris's behavior, at least no more than necessary. Plus, and maybe more important, Williams had read the New Testament and could quote parts of it from memory. If forced to, he could sound like an authentic religious authority.

2) Inform the press that you've changed—not just because you're unemployed and your wife has left you, but because something deep within you has been permanently altered for the better by the bad things you've done. Forged in the fire, chastened by sin, and all that. Morris began his media offensive in the pages of the *Washington Post*. "I am sort of making an effort not to work for bad people," he told the *Post* reporter. "I recently turned down a person who claimed to represent Imelda Marcos. I told them, 'You obviously take the reports of my foot fetish too seriously.'"

Some thought that Morris destroyed his own case by making a sex joke in an interview meant to convey his new attitude on life. This misses the point. Notice the subtle blame deflection in Morris's statements: I'm changing my life by changing my clients. In other words: It was never me who was bad. It was the people I worked for. Clever.

3) Send your spiritual adviser out to do interviews. I was one of the first journalists to talk to Williams about Morris, so I got the full, unrefined speech. "He is becoming a man of faith," Williams told me in earnest tones. "Our relationship has to do with what the meaning of life is." To encourage the process

of spiritual discovery, Williams said he had given Morris two books, *"Mere Christian,* by C. S. Lewis and the *Confessions,* by St. Augustine. I know he's read them."

The question I had was, Yes, but have *you* read them? (*"Mere Christian"* is in fact called *Mere Christianity.*) I never asked it. Williams was talking too fast, unpacking his rap about Dick the Seeker. "He can be in the middle of the night reading a book and he'll call me and say, 'Armstrong, you got to tell me, what does this *mean?'* He has all these questions: 'Why would God do this? How do you know when you're doing something wrong? How should I have known that it was wrong what I was doing?'"

My notes from the interview don't reflect a pause for laughter here, so I guess there wasn't one. Williams went on: "He's like a little kid who hungers for wisdom and knowledge. It's like what Dick says, 'Once you have been moved and you've seen part of the light, you can't ignore it, because you want to see the rest of the light.'" Williams even predicted that Morris, who was Jewish, was well on his way to becoming an evangelical Christian. "I've got a lot of hope for him. There's a lot there to work with. He's a decent guy. He's so honest, he's honest to the point he makes himself look bad. And when a man's honest, you can trust him. I'll tell you, that's the thing about faith."

Bill Clinton also understood "the thing about faith." At the depths of the Lewinsky scandal, when it looked like no one could save him, he called out for Jesse Jackson, who scurried over to the White House to lend his stamp of moral approval to the ailing president. It worked. It helped, anyway. No one will ever convince me that Clinton wasn't taking a page from his old pal Dick Morris's playbook.

Not everyone took such a cynical view of Clinton's post-Monica spiritual awakening. Some observers seemed to accept it at face value, just as they had Clinton's original denials of the affair. From the beginning, the scandal served as a kind of televised Rorschach blot: You could learn a lot about people by watching their reactions to it.

The week the story broke, I found myself on a show with Dan Rather. Rather, who had been delighted to milk the Simpson murders for every ratings point they might provide, suddenly had Profound Reservations about covering Monica. "I hate this story because I love my country," he said. Or something equally disingenuous to that effect. What a lie, I remember thinking.

Months later, I was sitting on another CNN set, this time with Frank Sesno. I don't remember what facet of the saga was unfolding that day (the stained dress? the grand jury testimony? the impeachment trial? There was so much), but I do remember that Sesno was excited to be covering it. "I love this fucking story," he said enthusiastically during a commercial break.

Sesno was hardly a Clinton hater or a member of the right-wing conspiracy. He was a journalist. A real newsman loves news and is honest enough to admit it. I felt blessed by the Lewinsky story from Day One, and not simply because I didn't like Clinton.

Thanks to the scandal, I saw and heard all sorts of fascinating things. On the very first day, I got to hear White House sycophant Sidney Blumenthal say with real conviction that "the president regards it all as bullshit, and it is." Weeks later I got to listen to a sitting congressman, Representative Bob Barr of Georgia, explain to a group of people at a party that, because of his chronic cocaine abuse, Bill Clinton has a permanent erection. When it was all over, I got to have dinner with Monica herself. She seemed nice enough, though whatever it was that Clinton saw in her remained invisible to me. I couldn't imagine her wearing a thong. I couldn't imagine wanting to see it.

Almost everything about the Lewinsky scandal was unexpected and deeply weird. But none of it was boring. For more than a year, I woke up every morning fully expecting something strange to happen.

One afternoon in the summer of 1998, I got a message at home from a British reporter named Allan Hall. Hall identified himself as the New York correspondent for the *Sunday Mirror* and asked me to call him back. He didn't say why, and I didn't think much of it. I've always liked British reporters. I've run into a lot of them while covering stories, and generally they're impressive: witty, well-educated, and physically brave. They're also frequently drunk. As a rule, a British reporter will begin boozing at the first opportunity, and won't stop until he passes out or you run out of money. I've rarely met one who didn't drink like a Soviet factory worker.

It has an effect on the product. British newspaper writing reads like a late-night conversation at the bar: bawdy, direct, packed with color and salacious tidbits. Not surprisingly, a lot of it is completely made up.

Allan Hall is the dean of late-night bar reporters. Even in England, Hall stands out for the over-the-top quality of his stories, most of them filed from the seamier fringes of American culture. "Don Johnson Weeps for Wife While Seducing Blonde in Booze Clinic," "Bill Gates Has an Insatiable Sex Drive," "Jacko's Wedding Album: He Wore Black and a Lot of Grease;

She Wore a Miniskirt"—Hall had his byline on all of them. For a while in the early 1990s, he covered the Lorena Bobbitt dismemberment trial, from which he produced a report with the memorable headline "Sliced Stumpy Works Again: Severed Penis Man Claims He Can Have Sex." Sometime later he switched to the fading-tennis-star-eating-disorder beat ("Billie Jean Binge Agony"). Allan Hall had been around.

Unfortunately, on the day he called me, I'd never heard of him. "What do you think of the Monica Lewinsky thing?" Hall asked. The interview was short and dull. I let loose with a few trite observations. He thanked me and hung up. I did think it was odd when an editor from the *Mirror* phoned my house from London a few hours later to ask where he should send the photographer to take my picture. But I ignored the call and went out to dinner. And that was it.

Until a week later, when I got a message from a friend of mine. "Caught your piece in the *Mirror*," he said. "Are you leading a double life?" He seemed to be snickering on the phone. Confused, I called him back, and before long I had the story in my hands. It had my byline on it. Identified as an "expert commentator," I had gone on for 750 words about Clinton's sexual technique—"a quickie here, a feel there, a grope somewhere else"—as well as his political prospects ("he lives to cheat another day"). The article became more overheated with every paragraph, and by the end the imagery matched the tone: "The house is on fire and the clock is ticking. Bill Clinton is medium-rare, scorched in places, but he will pull himself from the ashes."

Sure he will. Unless, of course, the lame duck's fair-weather friends take the impeachment bandwagon by storm. Or the jackboot of oppression sings like a canary. Or some other unlikely combination of clichés occurs. In that case, the piece predicted, "he really can go to the Big House for serious time."

Who writes like this? According to the *Mirror,* I do.

Pretty embarrassing. For a moment I considered calling the paper to make threatening noises. I'd had a similar experience a few months before when the *New York Post* had stolen an entire story of mine—removed my name, reworded a few sentences, and run the thing as original. Outraged, I'd called Bill Sanderson, the *Post* reporter whose name had been added to my piece. How could you do this? I yelled. "This is what we do at the *Post,*" he said. "I don't own my byline. They do. I do as I'm told. I like earning a salary from them." He didn't seem at all embarrassed. "I want to make somebody feel bad about this," I said. "Good luck," he replied, chuckling.

Somehow I suspected I'd be taken even less seriously by the *Mirror.* No reason to waste a transatlantic call on that, I decided. And anyway, I figured, it's not like anybody else I know is going to see it. Who reads the British tabloids?

For starters, British people. Within a day, a particularly florid selection from the piece was reprinted by the *Independent* in London. A week after that I got a call from a woman named Annette Witheridge at the *Scottish Daily Record* wondering if— as an expert commentator familiar to the British reading public—I'd like to share my insights into the Monica Lewinsky affair. Not a chance of that, I said. Let me tell you about a funny experience I recently had with another British journalist.

She didn't sound a bit surprised. Those are the perils of working with editors thousands of miles away, she explained. "Once the story gets to London, who knows what happens?"

The experience should have taught me not to take unexpected calls from people I don't know. But it didn't. From what

I've seen, at least half of all good stories originate from strangers who decide to call news organizations and reveal something interesting. You could do pretty well as a reporter just waiting by the phone.

One morning I got a call from a woman who claimed to know Monica Lewinsky. She sounded nervous and refused to give me her name. But she had some interesting things to say. Her daughter and Monica were in the same class in high school, the woman said, and for years she drove the car pool. A couple of times a week, she brought Monica to appointments with a woman in Beverly Hills named Irene Kassorla. Kassorla was a sex therapist.

That was the story. It was hard to believe it could be true. Monica Lewinsky went to a *sex therapist* in high school? It was almost too good. And the name "Irene Kassorla" sounded invented. I checked the listings in Los Angeles just to be sure. There she was. I left a message, and within an hour Kassorla called me back on her cell phone from an Italian restaurant in West Hollywood.

I could tell right away that she was going to be fun to talk to. After every third sentence she'd pause to take another bite of pasta. This was a good sign. If there's an iron law of journalism, it's that cautious people don't do interviews with their mouths full. Reckless people do. For my purposes, recklessness was good.

Kassorla didn't admit that Monica Lewinsky had been her patient. But she didn't deny it, either. Instead, she offered an unusually well developed theory of what happened between the president and the intern. Working in the White House, Kassorla said, "is like your first day of kindergarten. Can you imagine being this little kid in kindergarten and there's this nice daddy there? Your mommy has left you; she's gone home and told you to be brave. There are two hundred and fifty of you in the class, and all of a sudden the biggest daddy in the place takes you by the hand and shows you how to color, and shows you how to play with the clay, and shows you how to get on the tricycle, and when you fall he picks you up. I mean, it's pretty nice."

What a sick analogy, I thought. It got weirder.

"What intern in what country wouldn't if the top guy said, 'You're adorable, you're wonderful'? It's so seductive, it's so delicious to have a big daddy look at you. And then the thing develops. At first you think maybe he just wants to talk to you or something. It develops." Kassorla said that even she, a married woman in her mid-sixties, could see the attraction to Clinton. "I think he's cute. But if he and I did it, we'd have to have penetration. I'd insist."

The longer I talked to her, the more amazed I became that some professional licensing board had allowed this woman to see patients, much less high school students. If you had to pick the last person on earth you'd want to influence the psychological development of your teenage daughter, it would probably be Irene Kassorla.

Kassorla first came to national attention in 1980, when she published a sex manual titled *Nice Girls Do*. Based on Kassorla's own field work with her boyfriend, an editor at *Penthouse*, *Nice Girls Do* promised to take readers "beyond orgasm, beyond sexual gratification, and into sexual delight whenever you wish."

It was not a book for beginners. In order to reach the "untamable Maxi Orgasm" (comparable in intensity to a grand mal seizure), Dr. Kassorla prescribed gymnastic moves like the Bass Fiddle Position, as well as a grueling regimen of genital exercises. "Sex is a skill that has to be learned, practiced, and honed to precision," she wrote, and many book buyers seemed to agree. *Nice Girls Do* spent weeks on the best-seller lists, was translated into a number of languages, and eventually sold more than three million copies.

The book had a profound effect on many of its readers. I found one, a forty-eight-year-old electronics engineer named Steve Walz, living in Santa Cruz, California. Walz first read Kassorla's book in 1981. "My wife said, 'This doesn't look like much,'" he remembered, chuckling. "We turned out to be really wrong. This is no minor pop work."

For Walz it became more like a sacred text. After reading *Nice Girls Do*, Walz was transformed into an energetic apostle of Kassorlism, coaching scores of people (most of them young women) in the practical application of the master's teachings. His marriage soon fell apart, but Walz stayed true to his new beliefs. Late into the night, he studied Kassorla's theory of the cervical-pubococcygeal orgasm. He even worked to expand the literature of the faith, writing his own lengthy tutorial on cunnilingus. "It's a cause of mine," he said.

Walz is not alone. After he posted portions of Kassorla's work on the Internet, Walz said, "we had people calling up blubbering on the phone to thank her, and thank us for publishing her. She's had an incredible influence in the sexual awareness end of the counterculture."

According to Walz, Kassorlites are everywhere, walking clothed and unnoticed among us. When two of them meet, Kassorla's signature sexual technique serves as their secret handshake. "When a woman does that to you in bed," Walz told me, "you can just say the word 'Kassorla' to her and she'll know what you mean. You can bet she's read the book."

Irene Kassorla, Ph.D., was definitely a real sex therapist. But did she really know Monica Lewinsky? I called her back the next day to find out. She was warier this time. "My lawyer told me to say, 'I can neither confirm nor deny any association with any patient.'"

The interview might have ended there, but I could tell Kassorla wanted to keep talking. I guessed that she wanted to talk about the one thing virtually every person I've ever interviewed wants to talk about most: herself. So I asked her about her life. The floodgates opened.

"I'm the most amazing shrink," Kassorla said. "I'm the strongest, most effective shrink you ever saw. I know it. I have a gift. People kiss my hand sometimes when I go on the street. They say, 'Oh, you've saved my life.'" The secret to successful lifesaving, Kassorla explained, is her rapport with clients. "I have Kleenex in every room of my house because my patients come in here and they really spill their everything to me." Kassorla started crying herself just thinking about it.

Within minutes, she'd admitted that Monica Lewinsky had, in fact, been her patient for a number of years. Kassorla said some nasty things about Lewinsky's parents (pretty ungrateful, I thought, since they'd been paying the therapy bills), then implied that Monica had told her all about sex with Bill Clinton. "I have stories in my little head that would make your ears fall off," she said.

Unfortunately, she never shared them with me, mostly for fear she'd be subpoenaed. "This is my nightmare, that Ken Starr will find some loophole or something and come get me talking," she said, sounding worried. "I have a cushy life. I live in a bloody mansion here. I got a husband who thinks I'm fourteen. And if you think I want to be under Starr's glance or pressure, or be in

Washington when my patients need me, my life would be over. I'd be in the *Enquirer* as the crazy shrink who crazied the crazy."

I don't know if Irene Kassorla ever made the *National Enquirer*. She did figure prominently in the Starr Report. Not long after my story appeared, Kassorla was interviewed by investigators from the Office of the Independent Council. I felt a twinge of guilt when I found out. Then, years later, I saw a press release Kassorla had sent out, promoting herself ("Shrink to the Stars") on the basis of her relationship with Lewinsky. That made me feel better.

Deep down, I decided, Kassorla had probably enjoyed talking to Ken Starr's investigators—not because she wanted to betray Monica, but because it's human nature. Most people can hardly wait to reveal their secrets.

If you don't believe it, watch late-night television. Hang in long enough and you're likely to see an infomercial for toupees, complete with testimonials. "The girls at the health club used to laugh at me," one satisfied wig buyer will explain to the camera. "Not anymore." (Wait till they see this infomercial, I always think.) A half-dozen other guys in bad rugs will follow with their hard-luck tales of life before hair: "I couldn't get a date." "I was afraid to go shopping." "I was stuck in a dead-end job." In each case, a new hairpiece has been the answer.

This is confusing if you think about it. Why would these guys go to the trouble and expense of pretending they're not bald, only to go on television and talk about their fake hair? My theory: because they can't help themselves. They're compulsive self-revealers.

A lot of Americans are. A few years ago I caught a cab in downtown Los Angeles. We hadn't gone a mile before the driver launched into a monologue about all the unsavory people who have ridden in his car over the years: actors, drunken foreign businessmen, people who don't tip. The worst, he confided, are the politicians. "They're just the lowest," he said. "I mean, I cheat on my taxes, but those guys . . ."

It went on like this for half an hour, virtually every sentence revealing something new and embarrassing about the driver's personal life: how he'd once worked as a hash dealer in India; how his son, the one with the drug problem, had finally found happiness doing body piercing in Hawaii; how he himself still smoked pot from time to time, though increasingly he was turn- ing to concentrated ginseng oil for a more natural high. By the time we got to the hotel I was exhausted. "Here's my card," he said cheerfully, leaning over the seat. "Give me a call when you come back to town."

"Sure thing, chief," I said. "I'm being transferred to the IRS field office here next week. I'll look you up then."

Actually, I didn't say that, though I realized later I should have. Instead, I just took his card and thanked him for the insights. It's hard to know what to say when you're in the com- pany of a compulsive self-revealer. All you can do is listen.

And over the years I have: To the woman next to me on the plane who talked for an hour and a half about her husband's testicular cancer and subsequent nervous breakdown. To the car service driver who explained how he was committing adultery with his next-door neighbor. (He gave me his card, too.) To the hitchhiker I picked up outside Baltimore who informed me that although he'd had some "problems" with schizophrenia in the past, his time in prison seemed to have eased the symp- toms. And, of course, to countless tales of addiction, self-help, and recovery. A cabby once spent the entire trip from Capitol Hill to Georgetown reading me selections from his unpublished poetry.

What's most striking of all is how people divulge their secrets even when those secrets cast them in an unflattering light. Apparently, the urge to self-reveal is more powerful than the desire to look good. It must be. There's no other explanation.

Once, by pure coincidence, I wound up interviewing a man who had been my soccer coach when I was a child. I hadn't seen him since I was small, and before we got down to the point of the call, we chatted for a while. He mentioned his wife and children, whom I remembered well. Then, without warning, he began to unburden himself.

"Here's an interesting story," he began. "A couple of years ago this banker friend of mine told me about this beautiful girl, absolutely gorgeous. He said, 'Why don't you try her? She's terrific. She's a hooker.' And I said, 'Okay, that sounds great.' So I went to her condominium one night and . . ."

I didn't really want to hear the details. He provided them anyway.

People who've never tried it assume that conducting interviews requires some sort of special knowledge or talent. The real trick is staying quiet. If you let them talk, people will almost always tell you what you need to know, and usually much more. Journalism is really pretty easy.

Several years ago, I traveled through the Southwest with a senior member of Congress. The congressman in question was and is one of my favorite politicians in Washington. He's witty, smart, decent, and loves dogs. He's also, as I learned one afternoon in Dallas, completely bonkers.

"Hey, there's the grassy knoll," the congressman said, pointing out the window as we drove through Dealey Plaza. "Did you see that British documentary about the assassination that came on the other night about three? It was fascinating." I thought he was joking. By the time he finished explaining how Kennedy's autopsy photos had been doctored, I knew he wasn't.

Over the next hour, the congressman proceeded to give me the full story. The assassination, he said gravely, was in fact a planned "coup d'état" staged by "rogue CIA operatives" who killed the president and framed Oswald in an attempt to extend the Cold War. Or possibly to end it. The congressman wasn't sure which, though he did seem to have just about every other detail memorized.

But what about the physical evidence? I asked. Hasn't it been proved that Kennedy was killed with Oswald's gun?

He looked at me like I was an idiot. Speaking slowly, he explained the deception: Days before the assassination, CIA technicians fired a bullet from Oswald's gun into a pail of water. The slug was retrieved, coated with plastic, reloaded, and placed in a larger-caliber rifle, which was then used by government agents to kill Kennedy. The plastic coating disintegrated when the slug hit the president, leaving only the telltale marks from Oswald's rifle to throw off investigators from the Warren Commission.

Assuming, of course, that investigators from the Warren Commission weren't involved in the conspiracy, too. The congressman suspected they were. Just look at the FBI report on the crash of TWA flight 800 off Long Island, he said. "The government claims the plane just crashed on its own. You think that's really what happened?" Sure, I said. He shot me another

how-dumb-can-you-be? look. "I believed the Warren Commission, too," he said. "At first."

I never published what the congressman said—lucky for
him, every word was, by prearrangement, on background—but
I did take notes, mostly because I could hardly believe it was
really happening. Could this be the same man I'd seen speak
thoughtfully and coherently on the floor of the House of Representatives?

Yep. And he's not alone. No matter how many times I see it
happen, I'm always amazed by the bizarre and self-incriminating
things supposedly responsible people say to reporters. For a surprising number of public figures, sanity is only skin deep. There
are some serious eccentrics out there posing as normal citizens.

In the summer of 1998, *TIME* magazine asked me to
write a profile of Larry Klayman, the founder of Judicial Watch.
Modeled on the Ralph Nader blueprint, Judicial Watch was a
nonprofit "public interest" organization devoted to harassing its
ideological enemies with lawsuits. At the time, the group had
more than a dozen suits pending against various branches of the
Clinton administration, including the Justice Department, the
Commerce Department, and the FAA.

Klayman made particularly adept use of the rules of discovery. Over the previous few years, he'd deposed scores of Clinton
employees and supporters, from George Stephanopoulos to
James Carville's office assistant, as well as several journalists sympathetic to Clinton. At one point, Klayman hauled Paul Begala
into a six-hour deposition on the basis of a single joke Begala
told on C-Span.

Most conservatives (at least in theory) oppose using the legal
system to settle personal or political scores. Not Klayman. By

the time I interviewed him, he'd already sued his own mother in a financial dispute. Klayman seemed to realize the suit might earn him what a friend of mine once described as a "comma problem" in the press ("Larry Klayman, comma, who sued his own mother, comma, won the Nobel Prize today"). He defended it nonetheless. Taking your mother to court, Klayman said, is really an act of bravery and principle. He compared it to Reagan firing the air traffic controllers.

I arrived at dinner with Larry Klayman thinking I knew exactly what to expect. I put my tape recorder on the table and waited for some huffing about Monica Lewinsky. It never came. Klayman wasn't interested in talking about sex. He wanted to talk about another scandal—the *real* scandal—a conspiracy so diabolical, a cover-up so vast that its disclosure would turn Monica into a forgotten footnote. Klayman wanted to tell me about the murder of Ron Brown.

Brown, Clinton's commerce secretary, had been killed a couple of years before, along with a large number of reporters and businessmen, when his 737 slammed into the side of a mountain in Croatia. The 7,000-page Air Force report on the crash cited pilot error and bad air traffic control as causes. Klayman wasn't buying it. "Ron Brown was supposed to be deposed by Judicial Watch the week he went to Bosnia," Klayman said. "They may have sent him to Bosnia to keep him from being deposed."

Klayman looked directly into my eyes. "The hole in Brown's head looked an awful lot like a forty-five-caliber wound," he said. Thanks to pressure from "the White House, Joint Chiefs, Commerce and Transportation Departments," no autopsy had been performed, but some X rays of the body had been taken.

Unfortunately, those had since disappeared. "Nobody has them anymore," Klayman said with a knowing look.

This was getting crazy. I glanced at my tape recorder to make sure it was still running.

Klayman went on. "We know from pictures we've seen that Brown's body was very much intact. He was sitting at the back of the plane. He may have survived the crash. If he did survive, did a Croatian team that went up to the site, did they put him out of his misery for humanitarian reasons?"

My face must have registered some disbelief—the Croatians are working for the White House, too?—because Klayman soon changed the subject to his own experiences with Clinton's secret police. Lately, he said, "mysterious" people had been showing up at the offices of Judicial Watch. On several occasions, employees had been "followed home by people probably with various government agencies."

In other words: I know the conspiracy is real because I've seen it myself.

I left dinner believing I'd just witnessed a man's self-destruction. Larry Klayman, a person generally taken seriously by the world, had all but accused the White House of murdering the secretary of commerce. And he'd said it, not on hidden camera, but knowing that he was being recorded, which made it even stranger and more damning. It's one thing to have crackpot opinions, quite another to share them with the world intentionally.

I turned out to be wrong. Larry Klayman was not laughed out of Washington for his conspiracy theories. To this day, people continue to send donations to Judicial Watch. Klayman still appears as a guest on talk shows. We've had him on *Crossfire*.

(He becomes furious every time I ask him about suing his mother.) The point is, you can never tell how a story is going to be received.

You can be certain, though, that whoever you're writing about won't like the finished product. Just as everyone looks fatter on television, every story seems more negative in print, at least to its subject. In the summer of 1999, I finished a profile of then-governor George W. Bush for *Talk* magazine. I'd spent months interviewing Bush, talking to his friends, and traveling around the country with his presidential campaign.

By the end, I thought I understood him fairly well. Bush was witty and blunt, a bit of a towel-snapper but in a way I found charming. He was obviously a decent guy personally. And more than any candidate I'd interviewed, he seemed uninfected by the desire to win at all costs. I got the impression he could lose without being crushed.

I'd decided I liked Bush quite a bit, and all but said so in print. The night before I filed the story, I gave a copy to my wife. Her one question after she'd finished reading it was, "Aren't people going to think you're looking for a job in his administration?"

As it turned out, no. The story was not received in the way I'd expected it would be. On the day it returned from the printer, I was in a cab in Lower Manhattan when my cell phone rang. It was Jack Oliver, the deputy finance chairman of the Bush campaign. He was upset—so upset, I couldn't make out his words at first. "You fucked us!" he yelled. "I can't believe you did that. We gave you all this access, and you fucked us in return."

Bush hadn't liked the piece at all. In fact, I later heard from someone who was with him at the time, he was wounded by it.

He was surprised by a couple of faintly critical lines. (I'd pointed out that he dresses like someone who just got back from an afternoon of shoplifting at Sears.) He found the tone annoying. Most of all, he didn't like being quoted using profanity.

I don't think Bush was worried about the political ramifications. A couple of the other Republican candidates issued press releases attacking him for having a dirty mouth, but no one paid much attention. I doubt voters cared. Bush was bothered because he didn't think his quotes sounded like him. The words didn't square with his image of himself. As a friend of his explained it to me, it was like hearing yourself on tape for the first time and thinking: Who's that?

The micro-controversy probably would have disappeared within a few days had it not been for Karen Hughes, Bush's chief press aide. Hughes began telling people, including several friends of mine, that the quotes were false. I'd made them up, she said. Invented them, probably to get publicity for myself.

This was untrue. And Hughes knew it was untrue, since she was present during at least one of the interviews in which Bush used the *F*-word. The three of us had been in a small prop plane over Waco at the time. Hughes heard every word. There's no way she could have missed Bush saying "fuck." He said it several times in a very loud voice. According to campaign staffers, he said it all the time (and good for him). In any case, I had it on tape.

I called Hughes to demand that she stop slandering me. She said she hadn't. Moreover, Hughes claimed not to remember a single instance of Bush using foul language, ever, at any time. "The governor does not recall using that language," Hughes said robotically, over and over. "I've never heard him talk that way."

I wish I'd tape-recorded the call. Hughes's half of the conversation would have made a fascinating case study for an abnormal psychology textbook. The average person is incapable of lying with a straight face to someone who knows he's lying. It's too embarrassing; the charade is too obvious. There's no one to fool. Karen Hughes can do it without flinching. It doesn't seem to bother her at all. Which is either the mark of exceptional discipline or a mental condition. Maybe both.

Karen Hughes wasn't the first flack to attack one of my stories (though she may have been the most shamelessly dishonest). Most political pieces—particularly long, opinionated magazine articles—draw complaints. Ordinarily, this comes as no surprise. When you set out to write a hit piece, you expect the subject not to like the finished product. What is surprising—and what I've never been able to get used to—is hurting someone by accident.

In the spring of 2002, I decided to write a story for the *New York Times* about Tommy Jacomo, the longtime manager of the Palm restaurant in Washington. It was Tommy's thirtieth year at the Palm, a perfect occasion, it seemed to me, for a fawning profile. I'd known Tommy since I'd moved to Washington, and always liked him. He was friendly and witty and profane. In a city of careful people, he was flamboyantly colorful.

I soon learned how colorful. One of the first people I interviewed for the story made an offhand reference to Tommy's "cocaine trial." Confused, I checked the news clips. There it was: In 1977, Tommy Jacomo had been arrested for arranging the sale of an ounce of cocaine to an undercover DEA agent. The transaction had taken place inside the Palm. There was physical evidence, including a canceled check and at least one tape-recorded phone conversation. It was big news at the time. Tommy faced up to twelve years in prison. The prosecutor referred to him in the *Washington Post* as the "maître d' of cocaine."

Tommy didn't deny any of it when I asked him. He looked a little uncomfortable when the subject came up, but he also laughed as he recalled how Edward Bennett Williams had helped him beat the charges. Williams, the famed criminal defense lawyer and owner of the Washington Redskins, was a Palm regular. He and Tommy were after-hours friends who often went to the fights together in Atlantic City. Williams mobilized his law firm, Williams and Connolly, in Tommy's defense.

Ever sensitive to the racial politics of the city, Williams appointed a black attorney to defend Tommy. The lawyer's argument was that, while Tommy had indeed used and dealt cocaine in the past, he had not been involved in the sale at the Palm. In this case, the lawyer said, the federal government had set Tommy up.

Tommy himself never spoke in court. Considered too unpolished to take the stand (there were fears he'd light a cigarette or use the *F*-word) he sat silently through the trial, doing his best to look innocent and sympathetic. The jury acquitted him in an hour. Years later, one of the prosecutors in the case became a regular at the Palm. Tommy forgave him completely.

It was a great story. Plus, it had a moral: In Washington, everybody eats at the Palm—Democrats and Republicans, lobbyists and the lobbied, the defense and the prosecution. I thought it made Tommy look cool. I gave it prominent play in the piece.

It's hard to believe Tommy didn't know it was coming. But he didn't. His brother-in-law works in the *Times* printing plant in New Jersey, and he called Tommy's house at midnight when the paper came off the presses. I heard later that Tommy started crying on the phone when he learned the story mentioned his drug trial. Apparently, his two young daughters had no idea he'd ever been arrested. They'd gone to bed that night excited to see the story. Tommy had promised to tape it to the refrigerator in the morning. Now he had to hide the paper. He was humiliated. And really, really mad at me.

I discovered this around noon, when three different people called me from the Palm on their cell phones to report that Tommy was yelling my name, and not in a good way. A few days later, the *Hill* newspaper ran a story with the headline: "N.Y. TIMES STORY ANGERS JACOMO; Tucker Carlson persona non grata at Palm." (It was a slow news day.) The gist of the piece was, I was no longer welcome to eat in the restaurant.

I felt sick, and not just because I like the Palm's crab cakes. I'd accomplished precisely the opposite of what I'd set out to do. I'd insulted someone I'd meant to compliment, wounded a person I admire. It took the better part of a month, the intercession of several mutual friends, and a long boozy dinner to set things right with Tommy again. Even then I didn't understand how I could have so thoroughly misjudged the story. A cocaine arrest just hadn't struck me as that big a deal. Obviously, I have a blind spot.

So I can sympathize, and often do, with politicians who accidentally say stupid things in public. I felt sorry for Senator Trent Lott when he destroyed his own political career by making a dopey remark at Strom Thurmond's hundredth birthday party. Lott was never my favorite politician, but he's hardly the creepiest member of the United States Senate. And I don't think anyone believed he was actually pining for segregation when he said the country would have been better off if Senator Thurmond had won the 1948 presidential race.

Just as no one thought Senator Robert Byrd was intentionally using a racial slur when he uttered the phrase "white nigger" on a television show a few years ago. Everyone knew that Byrd was elderly and prone to strange outbursts. His words were understood as the ramblings of a doddering old man.

Harder to explain are Byrd's years as a recruiter for the Ku Klux Klan. Byrd's apologists imply that most southern men of a certain age were once members of the Klan, but that's simply not true. Joining the KKK was never the norm, anywhere. Nor did most southerners believe that black people were somehow morally unfit to defend their country in World War II. Byrd did, as he explained in a 1944 letter to Mississippi senator Theodore Bilbo, the most outspoken segregationist in Congress.

"Never in this world will I be convinced that race mixing in any field is good," Byrd wrote. "I am loyal to my country and know but reverence to her flag, but I shall never submit to fight beneath that banner with a Negro by my side. Rather I should die 1,000 deaths, and see Old Glory trampled in the dirt never to rise again, than to see this beloved land of ours become degraded by race mongrels."

Degraded by race mongrels? The letter alone doesn't disqualify Byrd from being taken seriously—people repent and change their views—but at the very least he should have to explain it. He never has. No one has ever pushed him to.

Trent Lott, meanwhile, couldn't stop explaining. Lott groveled before America in interview after interview, apologizing for what he'd said at Strom Thurmond's birthday, and promising to become a better human being. He came out for affirmative action. He pledged to spend more time with black people. He all but celebrated Kwanzaa on camera. None of it was enough. Crushed under the weight of the pile-on, he resigned as Senate majority leader, as everyone in Washington knew he would.

Partisanship as much as his own stupidity killed Lott's career, but stereotypes helped, too. Scandals generally go nowhere unless they confirm the public's preexisting suspicions about someone. If the pope were caught on tape tomorrow worshiping Satan, the story would likely die within a day. It would be too implausible. Video or not, no one would believe it.

But a Mississippi politician with secret racist views? Not a stretch for a lot of people, however unfair the assumption might have been in Lott's case. Scandals dogged Bill Clinton for eight years, not just because there was evidence he'd done things wrong (though often there was ample evidence) but because many people suspected he was capable of whatever he'd been accused of. Michael Jackson has had a tough time rebounding from child molestation charges for the same reason.

Representative Gary Condit was trapped by the same syndrome. There was never any evidence that he killed his girlfriend. He just looked like the sort of person who might have. Maybe it was his hair.

Condit also had the misfortune of winding up at the center of a story line with amazing (and from the perspective of the press, irresistible) parallels in recent history: a twenty-ish doctor's daughter from California comes to Washington as an intern, falls for a politician twice her age, and confides the details to an aunt who lives nearby. The politician denies the affair, then admits it. *Newsweek* documents a long pattern of womanizing. Before long, authorities are looking into charges that the politician has obstructed justice.

The similarities to the Lewinsky story were remarkable, made-for-TV-movie close. But I couldn't help being struck by the differences. Unlike Clinton, Condit faced his crisis virtually unarmed. He couldn't invoke executive privilege. He couldn't bomb Third World countries. His flacks were inept. He had no war room. He wasn't terribly clever or glib. His fellow Democrats had no political motive to defend him. Plus, his luck was terrible.

But that doesn't mean he murdered Chandra Levy. Consider the sum total of the evidence against Condit: Levy left her apartment for the last time without taking her handbag. This fact, according to political consultant and part-time criminologist Susan Estrich, was the key to the case: "The only two places I'd go without a purse," Estrich wrote in *USA Today,* "are the gym (which she had just quit) and the back of a motorcycle—something I don't ride, but Condit does."

There you have it: Condit did it. On his motorcycle. The proof is in the purse.

No wonder Condit was never arrested. Still, even though he was being destroyed by what was obviously the most unfair sort of speculation, no one in Washington seemed to feel sorry for him. His story evoked bad memories. The Condit scandal was like the straight-to-video version of the Lewinsky saga. Condit was Clinton played by an actor you'd never heard of. You almost expected him to have a porn star mustache.

Even the tabloid coverage had a grainy look. At one point, a supermarket tabloid reported that one of Condit's former girlfriends once found two neckties knotted together beneath his bed. This was offered as proof that Condit is a practitioner of "kinky sex."

Kinky? Chicken blood is kinky. Batman costumes are kinky. The "anal-oral contact" famously listed in a Starr Report footnote is kinky. But neckties? Maybe in Modesto. In Washington—resolutely square, no-casual-Fridays Washington—they're yesterday's sex toy.

Which may be the real moral of the story: Sexual snobbery was at work. News accounts portrayed Condit as a blow-dried cheeseball, a farm team pickup artist in polyester pants. For all the reports of his widespread womanizing, Condit never came off as a playboy. You couldn't picture him having an interesting affair, with travel and decent hotel rooms. It was easy to imagine him cruising for chicks in some racquetball club in central California.

And there were people who wanted you to imagine it. The Levy family for one. The D.C. police, for another. Both had motives to keep Condit in the news. The Levys wanted the police to continue searching for their daughter. Intensive press coverage, they realized, is always the quickest way to get police to act. Stories about sex and congressmen are the most likely to receive intensive press coverage. We only know that Condit and Levy had an affair because Levy's family confirmed it, then continued to feed the story with media interviews.

The police had an even more straightforward reason for tormenting Condit: ass-covering. The D.C. police department is legendarily bad. Washington cops bungle more investigations, solve fewer murders, get arrested for corruption more often, and shoot more people by accident than any American police department I'm aware of. Locally, they're a joke. (The good news is, they're rarely around, so you can usually drive as fast as you want in the District.)

Not surprisingly, the D.C. police completely screwed up the Levy investigation from the beginning. And that would have been the headline, if it weren't for Gary Condit. Condit gave the department perfect cover for its incompetence. Of course the Chandra Levy case hasn't been solved, the cops implied; Congressman Condit hasn't fully cooperated.

Except that Condit did cooperate, and about as fully as anyone could. He was questioned by investigators three times, with the juiciest details leaked afterward to the *Washington Post*. His apartment was searched. He gave a DNA sample. When the cops wanted to talk to his wife about his mistress, Condit set up the interview.

Still, police pretended not to be satisfied. So Condit underwent a polygraph test, given by an examiner with thirty-five years of experience in the FBI. He was asked if he had harmed Chandra Levy or knew where she was. He said no. The test indicated Condit was telling the truth.

The cops scoffed, dismissing the test as "self-serving" because Condit's attorneys set it up. A police spokesman said the department wanted a new test, this one administered by a current employee of the FBI. But if Condit had been able to beat one exam, as the cops suggested, why wouldn't he be able to beat another?

Good question. Not that anyone asked it. Not that it mattered. Condit never took another lie detector test. It wouldn't have helped him anyway. Condit's career in Congress was already over.

The next year, he was challenged in the Democratic primary by a former staffer with nearly identical political positions. Chandra Levy was the only issue in the race. Condit couldn't address Levy directly, since even the conversation was damning. ("When did you stop murdering your girlfriends?") He couldn't ignore it, since the scandal was all anyone wanted to talk about. His only option was not to speak at all. He lost the race by a wide margin.

Shortly before Condit returned to California in disgrace, Chandra Levy's remains were discovered in Rock Creek Park, in an area D.C. police had supposedly searched thoroughly several times. By this time, almost no one still believed Condit had committed the murder. A new suspect had emerged, a man being held for a series of violent attacks on joggers in Rock Creek Park. It was clear that Condit had been deeply wronged—by the press, by the police, by the Levy family, and by his colleagues in the House of Representatives, none of whom stood up for him. No one apologized.

We'll hear from Condit again someday. He'll make the "Where Are They Now?" edition of *People,* or some magazine show. A reporter will find him living alone in Modesto, selling real estate or teaching aerobics. He'll provide a few bitter quotes, and that will be it, the end of the public life of former congressman Gary Condit. His obituary will be mostly about Chandra Levy.

Looking back, it's hard to see what Condit could have done to save his career, apart from not having an affair with Levy in the first place. When you're a married member of Congress and your girlfriend disappears, sparking a high-profile homicide investigation, it's probably best to resign immediately and get busy studying for the Realtor's exam. Running for reelection is certain to be a waste of time. Condit was cooked from the beginning.

But not all sex scandals are cataclysmic. Most, particularly the ones that do not include a murder, are survivable. The trick is to stay calm, hire a good lawyer, and make sure you've got your story straight. And remember: No matter what they say, the police are not your friends.

Bob Beckel should have known all of this. As a veteran political consultant, he probably did know it but, in the heat of the moment, forgot to apply the principles of good scandal management. Whatever the cause, when it came time for his own sex scandal, Beckel dropped the ball. So to speak. His experience amounts to a primer on What Not to Do.

Beckel was once a prominent Democratic campaign manager (he ran Walter Mondale's 1984 White House bid), but by the summer of 2002 he was mostly a media figure. He was managing one statewide race that year, a long-shot Senate campaign in Idaho. The rest of the time he appeared on CNN as a political analyst and occasional guest host of *Crossfire*. He was also in the middle of a divorce.

One day in June, Beckel was home alone surfing the Internet. He came across the Web site for an escort service. One of the escorts, a twenty-three-year-old named "Tiffany," looked appealing. One thing led to another, and before long Tiffany was at Beckel's house in suburban Maryland. She stayed for two hours, working up a $600 bill. Before she left, Beckel made the first in a series of mistakes: He paid by check, and he bragged about himself.

Beckel told Tiffany that he was employed by a "major media syndicate." Tiffany was impressed. She asked Beckel if he would send her coded messages the next time he appeared on television. As it happened, the following night Beckel came on *Crossfire*, where we had a vigorous debate over the prescription drug bill. I didn't notice any cryptic phrases or hand gestures. Then again, I wasn't looking for them.

Two days later, Tiffany was back at Beckel's house. The bill this time came to $1,300 (leading one of Beckel's friends to point out that his real sin was causing inflation in the hooker market by paying twice the going rate). Again he paid by check. Then he left town for Idaho.

When he returned a couple of weeks later, there was a note on the windshield of his car. It was from Tiffany. She wanted $50,000. If Beckel didn't send the money, Tiffany promised to send "evidence of your illegal activities" to "your wife, your employer, and the newspapers." Tiffany clearly had the evidence. At home, Beckel found his own voice on his answering machine. It was a tape recording of his first call to the escort service.

It was at this point that Beckel made the worst decision of his life: He called the police.

The cops, of course, were very interested in Beckel's story. Tiffany and her pimp had apparently attempted blackmail before. The police asked him to put the details of his encounters with Tiffany—including the sexual details—in a sworn affidavit. For some reason, Beckel agreed.

Within days, the entire story was in the newspapers. Someone in the police department or prosecutor's office had leaked the affidavit, along with Beckel's name, spelled correctly. Beckel soon lost his consulting gig on the Idaho Senate campaign, as well as his job at CNN. His divorce, which was days from being settled, was suddenly reopened. His wife wanted full custody, not to mention more money.

Around this time, I ran into Beckel in an elevator. He looked terrible. He was sweating profusely. He smelled like stale tobacco. I felt sorry for him. Unsure of what to say, I asked the first question that popped into my mind: Was she cute?

"She was hot," he said. For a moment, he looked almost cheerful. Then he clammed up. "I'm under gag order," he said. "I can't talk about it."

But I knew he wanted to. Beckel was a talker. The year before, he'd told me all about his time in the federal witness protection program. During the 2000 presidential campaign, Beckel claimed, a group of Nazi skinheads had tried to assassinate him. Before the plot could be carried out, the government whisked Beckel off to a "safe house" in Arizona, where he lived for months in hiding "with two mob guys and a rabbi. The place didn't have air-conditioning. We just sat around and played cards all day. I think that's what broke up my marriage."

It was a preposterous story. Political consultants do not qualify for the witness protection program. And what was a rabbi doing in the safe house? It sounded like the setup to a joke. Beckel didn't look like he was kidding. He looked upset. He seemed to believe every word of what he had just said.

He looked the same way when we got off the elevator. As we stood in the lobby of the building, Beckel proceeded to explain the Real Story. What looked like a straightforward sex scandal (Talking Head Caught with Hooker) was in fact, he said, an elaborate "sting operation" gone awry. Beckel claimed that he had been working with the Montgomery County, Maryland, prosecutor's office to gather evidence against Tiffany and her fellow extortionists. In the end, the prosecutors betrayed him by releasing his name, which they'd promised to keep under seal. Beckel said he planned to sue.

Beckel dropped out of sight not long after our conversation. He told one reporter that he planned to leave politics for good, possibly to become an auto mechanic. I expect he'll resurface in Washington at some point, probably after a religious conversion.

Your Biggest Fan!

✳ ✳ ✳

I had just gotten off the *Crossfire* set when one of our producers handed me a stack of mail. On the way to the elevator, I glanced at it. On top of the pile was a registered letter from a law firm. It got my attention immediately. I've never had a pleasant letter from a lawyer.

This one was worse than most. It was written by an attorney in Indiana named Paul M. Blanton. Blanton wanted to let me know that his client, a woman named Kimberly Carter, was planning to file criminal sex charges against me in the Commonwealth of Kentucky. "Ms. Carter has informed me that she was raped by you," Blanton wrote. "If you should have any questions or concerns about any of the aforementioned, please do not hesitate to contact me."

Should I have any questions or concerns? I didn't know where to begin. Rape? Kentucky? Criminal charges? I knew I hadn't raped anyone. I didn't think I'd ever even been to Kentucky. The name Kimberly Carter sounded mildly familiar, though I couldn't recall why. I had the feeling that my life was about to change for the worse. I felt weak.

Then I noticed that the envelope had been opened. My producer had read the letter. She was looking at me in a way that made me uncomfortable, like she'd just discovered a terrible secret. Which I guess she had, but then so had I. I called her into my office and shut the door. I want you to know I didn't do this, I said, I promise. She looked relieved. "Of course not," she said.

I knew CNN wouldn't be as easy to convince. In fact, I knew the network would fire me immediately if it found out about the letter, and certainly if charges were filed against me in Kentucky. The one thing every journalist knows for certain about sex scandals is that they're always true. Partly true, anyway. Maybe you didn't rape this woman, they'd think; maybe you just had unusually rough sadomasochistic sex with her and she misconstrued it. Or maybe your affair with her simply fell apart in an acrimonious way, perhaps over your cocaine habit. Maybe you had sex with her but never knew her name. Something definitely happened between you, though. People don't just make up specific allegations out of nothing.

I went next door to see Bill Press, who was going through his own mail. I showed him the letter. He had two words of advice: "Bob Bennett." Bennett, who represented President Clinton during the early Lewinsky period, is the first lawyer most people in Washington think of when they hear the phrase "explosive allegations." For the scandal-besieged, Bob Bennett is almost a cliché. And for good reason. If you suspect you could be in deep trouble, there's no one better.

I finally reached Bennett on his cell phone an hour later. He was on a shuttle bus heading to the Hertz lot at an airport in the Midwest. He listened quietly. "First," he said, "don't worry. Second, don't tell anybody. I'll be back in town tomorrow. Call me."

I went home and went to bed. At three in the morning I woke up feeling completely out of control. Still half asleep, I was suddenly convinced that somehow I must have raped this woman, whoever she was. I must have done it while sleepwalking or during some sort of memory-erasing seizure. She couldn't have made up the whole thing. Maybe I have a brain tumor, I thought. Maybe I'm leading a double life I don't even know about. Maybe I'm going insane.

I got up and walked downstairs. For an hour I sat on the front steps thinking about my life, my wife and my three children, my job, and how it was all going to end because of something terrible I didn't even remember doing. I felt sadder than I had in a long time.

The next day, I found out more about what I had supposedly done. According to Kimberly Carter, whose lawyer relayed the details to Bob Bennett, I was in Louisville, Kentucky, one night two months before. Carter, an accountant who lives forty miles away in Mauckport, Indiana, was also in Louisville. We met at Harper's Restaurant on Hurstborne Parkway, where I slipped narcotics into her drink. By the time she awoke, she was covered with blood. She knew immediately that she had been violently raped. By me. In the restaurant. Presumably within view of dozens of other people, not one of whom had thought to report the crime to the police or the press.

It was a preposterous story. I'd never heard of Harper's Restaurant. I'd never been to Louisville. Judging from my schedule in March, I couldn't have gotten there. I was on television almost every night in Washington. Bennett explained this to Carter's lawyer, Paul "Matt" Blanton. Fine, said Blanton, prove it. In seven days, we're going to the prosecutor. By the way, he added, we have evidence that Carlson and my client know each other. There's correspondence.

Three days later, I took a lie detector test. If you've never been polygraphed, it probably doesn't seem like a very big deal, at least if you're innocent. You answer some questions as honestly as you can, and you leave. That's what I expected. I was wrong. Sitting through a polygraph exam is among the more unpleasant things I've ever done.

Bennett and I waited outside the conference room while the polygrapher set up his equipment. Bennett seemed jumpy. I think he believed me when I said I didn't rape anyone. On the other hand, he once worked for Clinton. He's learned not to take a client's explanation at face value.

The room smelled like a doctor's office as I walked in. Paul Minor, the former chief polygraph examiner at the FBI, greeted me with the solemn formality of an undertaker. Minor has been giving lie detector tests for more than thirty years—he's tested Anita Hill and Linda Tripp, among others—and he has the psych-out down cold.

"It's all right to be nervous," he began, as he tightened a black rubber strap around my chest to measure my breathing. "Most people are. There's a lot at stake or you wouldn't be here.

People are nervous about losing their jobs, or their reputations or . . ." He fixed his watery blue eyes on me. ". . . Going to prison. If you tell the truth, the whole truth, we'll be fine. If you don't, if you fudge at all, we're going to have problems."

I turned away from him to face the wall, and he began the control questions. "Do you drink coffee?" "Is today Monday?" "Are you in Washington?" It was unpleasant already.

Then he zeroed in. "Have you engaged in any sort of sex act with Kimberly Carter?" No. "Have you ever forced sex upon any female?" No. "Are you afraid of failing this polygraph?" No.

I mean, yes. I mean, I have no reason to fear failing, since I'm telling the truth, but I fear it anyway, just because failing it would be . . .

"Yes or no answers only." Yes. "Would you lie to me if you thought you could get away with it?"

Obviously this was the Zen part of the test. If I were guilty of something and I thought I could conceal it, I would lie. So in general the answer would be yes. Except in this case I wasn't guilty of anything and therefore wasn't planning to lie. I said no. The first time.

Minor took me through the entire list of questions two more times, throwing in an extra one ("Do you ever daydream about having sex with women other than your wife?") just to make me squirm. It worked. Ordinarily I'm not a very tense person, but by the end, I was drenched with sweat. I learned later that Minor once gave a polygraph exam to Woody Allen. I would have paid to see that. I can't even imagine the neurotic energy in the room.

Twenty minutes later I found out that I had passed the test. Bennett seemed jubilant, and very relieved. All that remained was to find out why Kimberly Carter was accusing me of a crime, keep the DA in Louisville from bringing charges against me, and prevent CNN from learning about any of it.

The following day, we solved the motive mystery. A private investigator had uncovered a letter from the Norton Psychiatric Center in Louisville concerning its patient, Kimberly Carter. Dated less than two years before, the letter referred to Carter's bipolar affective disorder as "a chronic condition requiring *strict* compliance to prevent symptom recurrence." Someone had forgotten to monitor her medication.

If I had been paying closer attention, I might have figured this out earlier. Carter had been writing letters and E-mails to me for months at CNN. Twice she had sent me small gifts, keychains, and ballpoint pens. I wrote her thank-you notes both times, hence her lawyer's claim about "correspondence." I hadn't remembered any of this. Later, one of my producers dug up an E-mail Carter sent me. "I watch your show all of the time," it said. "You are great." Carter wrote it on my birthday, a month after I supposedly raped her.

It's hard to hate someone who is delusional, and as angry as I was, I was inclined to give Carter a pass on grounds of craziness. Her lawyer, on the other hand, the weasely, pompous little Matt Blanton—I wanted to kill him. At the very least I wanted him to pay my legal bills, which by this point had reached over $14,000, not a dime of it covered by insurance or the network. And I wanted a prolonged, groveling, preferably tearful apology for sending a letter to my place of work accusing me of a felony sex crime.

I didn't get either one. Saul Pilchen, Bennett's able deputy, convinced me that suing Blanton for damages (and I was prepared to spend whatever it took to do it, as long as it wrecked his day) would only draw attention to the original accusation, discredited as it was. In the end, my name would be joined in the same sentence with the word rape, and it was worth at least fourteen grand to keep that from happening. Instead, Pilchen sent Blanton a tart letter pointing out that it's pretty irresponsible for an attorney to make such serious allegations based on the ramblings of a mental patient.

Blanton responded with a snippy letter explaining that his client had "decided to put this matter on hold at this time." As "a respected member and entrepreneur of Harrison County and other surrounding counties," Blanton wrote, Carter "understands very well the potential ramifications to her personal and entrepreneurial life" of a court case. In other words, Carter didn't want to embarrass herself by testifying against a rapist like me. It was infuriating.

Almost as infuriating as the letter Carter herself sent a week later. "I am glad to hear that Mr. Carlson can verify his innocence to the claim that I had made earlier," it began. "In light of the evidence that you provided to me, obviously the person who had assaulted me was not in actuality Tucker Carlson, but an impostor." She said sorry, sort of, and that was the extent of her contrition.

Because, as she went on to explain, she's the real victim here. "I don't appreciate the statements that you made about my mental status," Carter wrote, launching into a lecture about the need to show sensitivity and tolerance toward people with emotional disabilities. "I am a highly educated individual, with multiple degrees." Yes, she conceded, "I am a manic-depressive." But "everyone of concern knows that this condition can be very well managed. It is usually the ignorant that sensationalize it. There are some very successful people who have this condition. I know many."

In other words, Carter's craziness may have cost me thousands of dollars and jeopardized my career, my reputation, and my freedom. But it was still wrong of me—"ignorant"—to suggest that her mental illness might not be such a good thing. Nuts or not, Kimberly Carter had a lot of chutzpah.

Six months later, she wrote me again. This time she sent a clock radio with my name on it, along with a note apologizing "for the misunderstanding." A few months after that I got an Easter card from "Your Biggest Fan!" Her next card had five exclamation points, which I took as a sign of escalating mania. I looked her up on the Internet to try to assess the threat.

She was there. In fact, she had her own Web site, www. accounting-computing.com, complete with a photograph of herself sitting at the computer. I'd never seen her before. She was a heavyset woman in her early forties with waist-length hair and short bangs. She didn't look crazy.

People who stumble across her site probably never guess. Carter lists her many degrees (one in accounting, another in data processing, and yet another in something called Information Science) and promises to take care of just about any paperwork problem you might have. For reasonable rates, she'll draft your financial statements, process your Medicare claims, balance your books, or do your taxes. And although she doesn't say so, for no extra fee she's also happy to include you in her delusions.

The site gave me the creeps, and I was tempted to call her and tell her to stop bothering me. I never did, though. No matter how tempting it may be, no good can come from corresponding with the mentally ill.

I've concluded this after years of hard-earned experience. One of my first jobs in Washington was as the nut-mail editor of a quarterly magazine. It was a self-appointed position—nobody else wanted to assume it—but in its own way a rewarding one. As NME, I took calls and read letters from people upset over our editorial stands: conspiracists, Libertarians, men with strange accents ranting about obscure ethnic conflicts ("I can assure you that the Kazakh people will not abide this blood libel. . . . ") and so, obsessively, on.

It started out as a fun job, but even nut mail gets boring if you read enough of it. To keep myself amused, I began writing back. Baiting crazies is a mean thing to do. Even at the time I recognized that. But I couldn't help myself. So I assured the mad scientist in Baltimore that his Alternative Theory of Gravity really did make sense. I told a number of framed-by-the-Man prison inmates that we'd begin investigations into their cases. And I stoked countless conspiracy theories.

About one out of every three nut mailers is obsessed with the CIA in one way or another, so I had plenty of opportunity to hone a reply. It came in a couple of forms. The first was the empathy note:

Dear Mr. Jones,

Thank you for your important communication, which we received this morning. It was nice to find at least one reader who comprehends THE TRUTH about the CIA and President Kennedy. [Nut mailers appreciate it when you write back in all caps; it lets them know you UNDERSTAND.]

But what you may not realize is that the plot was actually larger than you've suggested. The Mafia was paid for its work not simply with gold bullion smuggled into Miami by Cuban intelligence, but also with cash supplied by a little-known paramilitary unit from within the Federal Reserve known as Omega Division. It was Omega Division that Jim Garrison was alluding to when he . . .

They loved it. I'd get even longer letters back thanking me for the information, or invitations to come out to Michigan some time so we could talk more about it.

The other draft of my CIA letter wasn't as popular with the nut mailers. I thought of it as the even-paranoids-have-enemies version. It began like this:

Dear Mr. Jones,

Your recent letter to the editor has been noted with some dismay here at Langley. According to our files, this is not the first time you have divulged details about the Agency's methods and practices in a public forum. Recent surveillance conducted from within your brain also suggests that you have continued to have unauthorized thoughts, despite repeated warnings from the Directorate. Please be aware that if you do not desist immediately, we will be forced to increase the severity of your headaches . . .

I always felt a twinge of guilt when I sent that one, not that it stopped me.

I wouldn't send a letter like that today. Made-up stories have unintended consequences, I've learned again and again. My first experience with the downside of fiction came during my senior year in college, when I tried to help one of my roommates who had wound up in trouble with an economics professor. As was his custom, my roommate hadn't bothered to show up for a single class all semester, assuming he could learn all he needed to know in forty-eight coffee-soaked hours and do decently on the exam. Days before the midterm, he got a call from the professor. "Just thought you'd like to know," she said, "I've counted each one of your absences against you. No matter how well you do on the test, there's no way you can pass the course."

My roommate was stunned, and once I heard about it, so was I. Failing a class simply for doing no work? Outrageous. We decided to come up with an excuse. But what could explain a semester's worth of missed economics classes? A death in the family seemed a bit dramatic. Imprisonment struck us both as self-discrediting. In a flash, it came to me: emotional instability. Perfect, we agreed.

My roommate found a book on abnormal psychology, I sat down at the keyboard, and we got to work. It wasn't easy to settle on an affliction. We scanned the index. Agoraphobia? Too obscure. Schizophrenia? Too scary. Chronic fatigue syndrome? Too hard to explain. We settled for something that sounded grave but not dangerous: acute neurotic depression.

"Dear Professor," began the letter, which was signed by a fictitious psychologist from Maryland, "I am writing to you on behalf of a patient of mine who is also a student of yours." The psychologist had very official-looking stationery, and he seemed to take an almost avuncular interest in my roommate, Bill.

Bill, the shrink explained, had loads of problems. In addition to being a suicidal alcoholic, Bill still bore emotional scars from growing up amid "maladaptive family patterns." Bill's behavioral symptoms, the psychologist wrote, amounted to "a textbook example of acute neurotic depression."

And indeed they did, since we copied them verbatim from the textbook: "Bill has difficulty concentrating, exhibits high levels of anxiety and apprehensiveness, together with diminished activity, lowered self-confidence, constricted interests and a general lack of initiative."

I remember chuckling as I typed the letter, sure it would reduce the professor to weepy sympathy. But just to be sure, we ended on a note of hope: "Fortunately, Bill has responded well to a combination of antidepressant and anti-anxiety drugs. He is also attending Alcoholics Anonymous. I am in regular contact with Bill, and believe that his chances of recovery are good."

Good, but not a sure thing. The last paragraph was pretty explicit about the role a college professor could play in Bill's personal recovery process: "The road to wellness is a long one, but I believe that, if given the chance, Bill can rise above his recent past. Of paramount importance are instances in which he can meet success in tangible ways. He is an impressive and likable young man who needs opportunities to redress his mistakes. I hope that this letter has made Bill's situation clear and you will show him the sensitivity that his full recovery requires."

That ought to do it, we thought.

We were right. Within about two hours, the dean of students had summoned Bill to his office and kicked him out of school.

What had seemed to us like a clever excuse looked to college administrators like cause for immediate hospitalization, not to mention a potential liability nightmare. They could picture Bill heading for the bell tower. The dean told him to pack his bags and be off campus by nightfall. "We just don't have the facilities to meet your needs," he said with what Bill later told me sounded like genuine sadness.

It was another three years before Bill got his undergraduate degree. Everything worked out in the end, though. He graduated at the top of his class from a famous law school. (I was in the front row when he got his diploma, the most relieved person in the room.) As I type this, he is making important decisions in his own rather large office in the executive branch of the federal government.

The Other Tucker Carlson

✳ ✳ ✳

After years of writing political stories for newspapers and magazines, I thought I knew all about hostile responses from the public. Then I went into television. For pure red-in-the-face, neck-bulging, I-know-where-you-live-buddy reactions, nothing beats TV. It brings out the crazy in people.

In the spring of 1996, I went on Chris Matthews's show to talk about Ross Perot, who was running for president that year and whom I'd been covering. On the air I made the point—in a subtle way, I thought—that Perot might not be all there, a few tacos short of a combo platter. At the time, it didn't seem like an outrageous thing to say.

Indeed, Perot himself had already made a compelling case that he was unbalanced. Four years before, during a televised debate, he had informed America that he was a marked man.

"The Vietnamese," he said, "sent people into Canada to make arrangements to have me and my family killed. The most significant effort they had one night is five people coming across my lawn with rifles." Perot later explained that the Communist insurgents were expelled from suburban Dallas by his own crack security team using only a German shepherd, which "worked them like a sheepdog," biting one of them as he ran off into the night. In retrospect, it is surprising Perot did not see the assassins with his own eyes since, as his former security consultant told the *New York Times,* Perot "would sometimes prowl the grounds himself, armed with an automatic rifle." .

Given the evidence, I felt my remarks were justified, even understated. Others didn't agree.

By the time I got back to my office, there were a dozen angry messages on my machine. One stood out as particularly enraged—I could almost feel the woman shaking with fury as she spoke. So I called her back.

She started yelling immediately. Who did I think I was? she wanted to know, and where did I get off saying something like that, and just how did I get to be such a repulsive, reprehensible person? I made a game attempt at answering, but she cut me off. You say Ross Perot is crazy? she screamed. "*You're* crazy."

I *am?* I thought. How do you know? "I'm a psychologist," she said. Her name was Pat Cummings, and she claimed to have a practice in suburban Maryland. *That's* how she knew I was crazy. And, she explained, not crazy in a good way. *Bad* crazy: delusional, vicious, sociopathic. Evil, really.

Well, I said, since you're a psychologist, you'll definitely want to get some treatment for that anger problem of yours. Then I signed off. Talking to Dr. Cummings was starting to depress me.

Not that I really believed her. A real psychologist wouldn't talk that way. No actual licensed mental health professional would call a total stranger "crazy." What if I'd taken her diagnosis to heart and had myself committed? Or gone to sleep with my head in a dry cleaning bag? No, the more I thought about it, the less I believed her. Pretending to be a shrink, I figured, must be the modern version of a Napoleon complex.

Four days later, I ran into Pat Cummings again. This time she was staring at me from a monitor in a television studio. I'd shown up to talk about Ross Perot again. So, it turned out, had she. Only, as a cameraman explained, she had refused to share a set with me and so was doing the interview by remote from another studio upstairs in the building. "Pat Cummings, Ph.D.," I soon learned, was both a real psychologist and a Perot volunteer.

On-air discussion that night never touched on our previous chat, and though I wanted to reminisce, Dr. Cummings must have slipped out the back door, because I never saw her again. Months went by, and my memory started to fog. Could the genuine psychologist on television really have been the same person who called to scream at me? I began to doubt it, and before long Pat Cummings left my thoughts entirely.

Months later, she reappeared. Over breakfast one morning, I was amazed to find Dr. Cummings lurking in the second paragraph of a David Broder column in the *Washington Post*. Identified as a "clinical psychologist and independent candidate for the Maryland legislature," Cummings was quoted extensively, claiming that "Ross Perot is not crazy." "In fact," she assured readers of the *Post,* "he could be included in a study of exceptionally healthy individuals." Sounded like the same woman to me.

Still, I had to be sure. So I called her. She confirmed not only her identity but also my diagnosis: still crazy after all these months. As she explained it, I was "a person who lacks conscience and an ability to interact in a responsible and ethical way in this society." Just in case I didn't understand the clinical definition, she reduced it to layman's terms: "Look, I have no respect for you . . . I think that you are a person of very low character."

Interesting, I said. May I quote you on that? Even over the phone line, I thought I could hear her mind begin to imagine the consequences: a trip to the professional review board, charges of irresponsible conduct, punishment. "Are you going to now try to cost me my license?" she demanded, sounding a shade less confident.

In fact, I did try. The next day I dropped a note to the Maryland Board of Examiners of Psychologists suggesting that someone examine Dr. Cummings. No one ever wrote me back. She is probably still practicing. I hope her patients don't mention Ross Perot during their sessions.

The problem with being attacked for what you say on television is that it's personal. When you write a magazine story and people get mad, you can tell yourself that what they're really mad about is the story. They just didn't agree with it. When you're assaulted after a television appearance, there's no pretending. The attack is aimed at you, the person. There's something about you that somebody else finds offensive, loathsome, repulsive. It can hurt your feelings.

For the first couple of years after I signed with CNN, it occasionally hurt mine. I quickly gave up trying to defend myself. Addressing the specifics of a complaint took too long and, in the end, wasn't very emotionally satisfying. Instead, I began responding with a form letter, which I kept ready on my desktop:

Dear Mr. Jones,

    Fuck you.

Sincerely,

Tucker Carlson

I sent scores of those, until one day a guy wrote back to say he was going to contact the FBI. He didn't explain on what grounds (interstate swearing?), but I decided that using profanity wasn't worth the trouble, rewarding as it was. My new form letter sounded like a form letter, like the sort of insultingly banal computer-generated response you might get if you wrote the White House asking to be appointed secretary of agriculture:

Dear Mr. Jones,

    Thank you for your interest in employment opportunities. Unfortunately, there is nothing available at this time in your area of interest. However, I am confident that with your impressive credentials you will secure an excellent position elsewhere.

    We will keep your correspondence on file, and keep you in mind if the staffing situation changes in the future. Best of luck.

Sincerely,

Tucker Carlson

It was the most confusing letter I could think of. Unfortunately, it only increased the volume of hostile mail. Viewers often wrote back to explain that they hadn't been looking for a job, they just wanted to tell me how much they hated me. So I'd have to send it again. It was a self-defeating cycle.

185

Not to mention time-consuming. I didn't solve the problem of hostile mail until I finally understood the nature of the people who send it. They are essentially nonconfrontational. (The confrontational ones are the ones who show up at your house.) That's why they've chosen to pour out their hostility to someone far away they've never met. They enjoy getting mad at someone who won't talk back. They're timid people. They fear contact most of all.

This isn't just a theory. For several years, I've conducted an experiment to prove it. I reply only to the most bellicose letters and E-mails, the ones that imply violence or degenerate into hard-to-understand rants. The ones where you can almost hear the writer pounding on his keyboard. I respond with what I think of as the Cell Phone Bluff: "Thanks for writing. Here's my cell phone number. Please call me so we can talk." No one has ever called.

Of course, if anyone ever does, I'll have a problem. I'm not that interested in being yelled at by someone I don't know. My plan at that point is to invent a reason to get off the phone quickly but, before I do, offer to continue the exchange on-line. As proof of my sincerity, I'll divulge my supersecret, close-friends-only E-mail address. Only it won't be mine. It will be an E-mail address for the other Tucker Carlson.

And there is one. I first became aware of his existence several years ago, when I got a call from a guy I was writing an unflattering story about. "We're going to turn the tables and do a little research on you," the man said. "I was interested to note that your father is quite progressive on social issues." He is? I said. Yep, said the man. "Your father is Arne Carlson, the former governor of Minnesota. And he's pretty liberal. How did you get to be so right-wing?"

I had no idea what he was talking about. I soon learned. Apparently, the man had punched my name into an electronic database of news stories and come up with articles about Governor Carlson's oldest son, who is about my age and whose nickname is Tucker. Another Tucker Carlson. What a weird coincidence, I thought.

A few months later, I went to New York to give a speech to a Republican women's club. The group's president greeted me like an old friend. "I knew your grandmother," she said. "She was a lovely person." Thank you, I said, wondering how my grandmother, who lived in Hawaii for most of her life, had found time to strike up friendships with New York Republicans.

Before I could ask, another woman approached to explain the night's speaking format. I had forgotten to fax her a bio, but she seemed to know a lot about me. "Did you ever marry Emery?" she asked. No, I didn't, I said, totally confused but trying to be polite. She looked crestfallen. "Well, that was so romantic," she said, "how you dedicated all of that to her. I just wanted to know how it turned out."

I smiled, unsure of what to say. She tried to comfort me. "With all your experience as a disk jockey, I know you'll do great tonight."

It was becoming clear there had been some sort of terrible misunderstanding, but I decided to ignore it. I was almost to the dais when the woman threw out one last compliment. "I really admire the work your father is doing," she said. A blank expression must have come over my face, because she did her best to jog my memory. "You know, your *father,* the governor of Minnesota."

There was no avoiding it now. As I explained my lack of connection to Arne Carlson, the woman who had said she knew my grandmother glared at me, as if I'd somehow lied about my heritage. The other woman just looked panicked. "But I've written a long introduction for you," she said, waving a sheet of paper in my face. ("Tucker Carlson was born into politics," it began.) "I need something else to say. Give me a couple of sentences, and I'll write them down verbatim."

No problem, I said, and began dictating: "Tucker Carlson, a world-renowned newspaper and magazine journalist, has been awarded the Victoria Cross for gallantry."

The woman scribbled furiously. She got to the end of the sentence, paused ("Two *L*s in 'gallantry'?"), then abruptly stopped. Suddenly, she looked very irritated.

Everything turned out all right in the end. Ann Coulter, who spoke after me, spent a good portion of her speech attacking abortion. There's no more pro-choice group in the world than affluent Manhattan Republican women, who tend to see abortion as not simply a right, but an excellent way to keep the black population under control. The crowd was so offended by Coulter's remarks that by the time we sat down for dinner no one seemed to remember I was an impostor. I didn't forget, though. I returned to Washington determined to learn more about the other Tucker Carlson.

I soon found all I needed to know in his mother's autobiography, titled *This Broad's Life*. Barbara Carlson concedes on the first page of the book that this broad's life has been one long train wreck. She goes on to chronicle her addictions to pills, booze, and snack food, and her extended recoveries from all three. She writes about her incontinence, her affairs, her cosmetic surgery, her love of oral sex, her digestive problems, and the tattoo on her butt. Worst of all, she writes about her family.

I've never liked Arne Carlson—he yelled at me once during an interview—but I felt sorry for him by the end of the book.

Not only is his former wife unstable, in and out of mental hospitals for decades, but she is physically dangerous. She boasts about smashing him in the face with a cast-iron frying pan and stabbing him at least twice, once with a knife. Then she blames him for her violent outbursts. During their marriage, she writes, "he never once touched my vagina with his hand."

And that's complimentary compared to what she writes about her son. Tucker, she explains, is a loser. After graduating from "a technical college near Minneapolis," he attempted to start a real career, "but quickly discovered he could make more money spinning records and emceeing mud wrestling in strip clubs." He was working in a bar in North Carolina, dating an exotic dancer, when his mother called to say that his grandmother had died.

"Tucker took the news very badly," Barbara writes. "He stayed [in North Carolina] for a club's grand opening, and by the time he got to the airport to fly home for the funeral, he was sleep-deprived, nauseated, and stinking drunk. He piled three hundred $1 bills on the counter to pay for his ticket (he was always paid in $1 bills that came from the strippers' tips at the club) and passed out in the rest room on the plane."

Imagine being dragged unconscious from an airplane lavatory. Now, imagine your mother telling everyone you've ever met about it in her book. That's what it's like to be the other Tucker Carlson.

Years later, I got an E-mail from a guy who'd gone to high school with the other Tucker Carlson. He'd read one of my stories and was delighted to find that I'd finally gotten my life together. He sounded pleased and—I could tell by his tone— more than a little surprised. Congratulations, he said.

I wrote back and thanked him profusely.

Afterword

The new version of *Crossfire* lasted almost exactly a year. In mid-April 2003—tax day, as it happened—the show was cut in half, from an hour to thirty minutes, and moved to 4:30 in the afternoon. I got the news on my cell phone while walking through the Indianapolis airport. It was a short conversation.

Some things are simply impervious to spin or euphemism: Death. Imprisonment. Having your show bounced from prime time to the late afternoon. It's bad. There's no pretending otherwise. The president of the network tried to be nice about it. He even mentioned something about "new opportunities" for the show, though it wasn't clear what those might be.

Others were more direct. By the time I got home, my picture was on the Drudge Report, beneath the unpleasantly accurate headline: "Downgraded." More indignities followed. On our first day in the new time slot, the traditional plate of cookies—chocolate chip, often with macadamia nuts—was missing from the greenroom. From now on, we were told, guests on *Crossfire* would have to do without their preshow snack.

And that was just the beginning. After the show, we discovered that our box of baby wipes—essential for removing TV makeup—was gone. In its place was a note from the makeup artist, who had already left and gone home: "Use soap in bathroom w/ tap water. Sorry."

Under the circumstances, it was hard not to take these as indicators of our impending demise. No one ever explained exactly why *Crossfire* had been moved. No one promised it wouldn't be moved again or eliminated altogether. Cookies and baby wipes suddenly began to look like ominous signs. Maybe they were. As I learned on *Spin Room,* a mug is never just a mug. Except when it is.

The point is, you can't know. No one knows what's going to happen tomorrow, including the people planning for it. In television news, there's no future, only now. It took me about twelve hours to become a talk show host. In the years since, I've realized I could become an unemployed talk show host a lot quicker.

I try not to spend too much time worrying about it. I care, of course, just not too much. That was Larry King's advice. And from where I sit, Larry King looks like one of the wisest men in the world.

Tucker Carlson

Washington, D.C.

June 2003